ALL CHURCHES GREAT AND SMALL

60 ideas for IMPROVING your church's ministry

ALL CHURCHES GREAT AND SMALL

60 ideas for IMPROVING your church's ministry

KIRK AND ROSIE FARNSWORTH

JUDSON PRESS
PUBLISHERS SINCE 1824

Valley Forge, Pennsylvania

ALL CHURCHES GREAT AND SMALL
60 Ideas for Improving Your Church's Ministry

© 2005 by Judson Press, Valley Forge, PA 19482-0851• All rights reserved.

No part of this publication may be reproduced, stored in a retrieval system, or transmitted in any form or by any means, electronic, mechanical, photocopying, recording, or otherwise, without the prior permission of the copyright owner, except for brief quotations included in a review of the book.

Judson Press has made every effort to trace the ownership of all quotes. In the event of a question arising from the use of a quote, we regret any error made and will be pleased to make the necessary correction in future printings and editions of this book.

Unless otherwise noted, Scripture quotations in this volume are from the Holy Bible, New Living Translation, copyright © 1996. Used by permission of Tyndale House Publishers, Inc., Wheaton, IL 60189. All rights reserved.

The Amplified Bible, Old Testament. Copyright © 1962, 1964 by Zondervan Publishing House. Used by permission. (Amplified Bible, Old Testament).

The Amplified New Testament, © 1954, 1958, 1987 by The Lockman Foundation. Used by permission. (The Amplified New Testament).

The Holy Bible, King James Version. (KJV).

The Message. Copyright © 1993, 1994, 1995. Used by permission of NavPress Publishing Group. (The Message).

The New American Standard Bible, © 1960, 1962, 1963, 1968, 1971, 1972, 1973, 1975, 1977 by The Lockman Foundation. Used by permission. (NASB).

HOLY BIBLE: New International Version, copyright © 1973, 1978, 1984. Used by permission of Zondervan Bible Publishers. (NIV).

The New King James Version. Copyright © 1972, 1984 by Thomas Nelson Inc. (NKJV).

The Living Bible, copyright © 1971. Used by permission of Tyndale House Publishers, Inc., Wheaton, IL 60189. All right reserved. (TLB).

The Modern Language Bible: The New Berkeley Version in Modern English copyright © 1945, 1959, 1969 by Hendrickson Publishers, Inc. Used by permission. All rights reserved. (Berkeley).

Library of Congress Cataloging-in-Publication Data
Farnsworth, Kirk E.
   All churches great and small : 60 ideas for improving your church's ministry / Kirk and Rosie Farnsworth.— 1st ed.
     p. cm.
   Includes bibliographical references and indexes.
   ISBN 0-8170-1478-0 (alk. paper)
   1. Small churches. I. Farnsworth, Rosie. II. Title.
   BV637.8.F375 2005
   253—dc22

                                                                    2004026737

Printed in the U.S.A.
11 10 09 08 07 06 05
10 9 8 7 6 5 4 3 2 1

This book is lovingly dedicated
to everyone in The Gathering Church,
every one a minister.

contents

acknowledgments

Our friends and family members who are pleasantly intrigued by, faithfully praying for, and generously giving to the work the Lord is doing in and through our unique little church called The Gathering. Their thoughtfulness is very uplifting and much appreciated. Our younger son, Eric Farnsworth, said it perfectly: "To honor you, we honor your ministry."

Lisl Helms for her dedication, expertise, and grace while under pressure to meet deadlines at every stage of typing the manuscript.

Randy Frame, Acquisitions Editor, Judson Press, for his wisdom and gentle prodding in making our book understandable and useful to the reader.

Dr. Casey Williams, Managing Editor, Judson Press, for her caring expertise in guiding the project through to completion.

Rev. David Passey, Northwest District Superintendent, Missionary Church, for his encouragement and support of our biblical understanding of what a church should be.

Rev. Tom Swank, then Director of Discipling Ministries, Missionary Church, for his help in resourcing our small-church survey.

Other pastors, denominational leaders, and partners in ministry who have been a special encouragement to us: Rev. Ernest Batten, Dr. Dan and Jessie Hayden, Joe Helms, Dr. John Moran, Rev. Marc Pearson, and most especially the people of The Gathering Church, whom God has given us to share in this wonderful journey of faithfully and fruitfully being the church that God has designed us to be.

introduction

Our passion is small churches.

- We prize the advantages small churches have because of their size.
- We embrace the small, faithful churches where God gets all the glory.
- We love the creativity that is evident in the DNA of small, faithful, healthy churches.
- We celebrate the future of small, faithful, healthy, great churches.

We believe that faithfulness, not bigness, leads to greatness! We also recognize that many smaller churches are not faithful, nor are they healthy. The same holds for bigger churches. Churches of every size and type have turned their back on God's desire to give them his kingdom. Consequently, we are seeing a near-epidemic of bored people walking away from irrelevance, and burned-out pastors giving up because of apparent ineffectiveness.

Some smaller churches are in serious trouble because they are unwilling to change and unable to grow. Is that true of your church? Or is your church small not because of fatalistic resignation or demographic default but because of kingdom-oriented choice? Does your church have the potential to be creative in reinventing itself so that it can be a healthier church?

Our purpose in writing this book, first, is to uphold God's desire specifically for small churches and to uncover his design for their faithfulness, their health, and the greatness of their resourceful, worldwide ministry. Second, it is our intention to challenge the assumption that what works for big churches should be the norm for all churches. Third, we will challenge small churches that do not enjoy kingdom work and dare them to reinvent creatively the tradition-bound structures and procedures that steal their joy.

All churches can be great, but small churches have the advantage. We feel it is time to celebrate the fact that small churches actually have an abundance of genuine advantages. It is time to proudly proclaim: Smaller is better!

We will devote the majority of our attention to these ten areas of biblically life-transforming activities:

1. Shepherding the flock with the top priority of knowing the state of your flock and putting your heart into its care.
2. Gathering together into God's presence for his purpose.
3. Covenanting in love and faithfulness to promises with a common purpose.
4. Ministering in response to being equipped for spiritual gifts–based ministry.
5. Studying to make responsible decisions to live as Jesus lived and to be his disciples.
6. Worshiping with the sacrifice of praise and with humble adoration to an awesome God.
7. Praying in one accord to claim victory in Jesus and enforce the victory of light over darkness.
8. Giving through generous living and simple living, always remembering to put God first.
9. Living in the Spirit by dying to self-centeredness and living with Spirit-filled fruitfulness.
10. Witnessing for the purpose of adding new believers and churches to the kingdom, while acting with urgency and abiding in discipleship.

These life-transforming activities are vital to the health of your small church. Near the beginning of Chapters 3–12, we provide summary statements of *how the small church has the advantage.* (We preview them in Chapter 1.) Several small-church advantages are also presented in the first two chapters, including the results of two major empirical studies. These results are huge: Small churches outperform larger churches in *five of the ten* vital qualities of strong churches (mid-size churches have the advantage in only one, and large churches zero—none, nada) and in *seven of the eight* essential qualities of healthy churches. You can look up all thirty-three advantages in the Small-church Advantages index at the end of the book.

What people do (including the pastor) in church will determine whether it is a healthy church. If they are faithfully involved in life-transforming activities and efforts, they will be healthy people and the church will thereby be a healthy church. Of course, both transformation and health are matters of degree. But to whatever extent we want to talk about a healthy church, we must talk about the spiritual health of the people, whatever their degree of transformation may be. They rise and fall together.

It is our hope that you will be greatly encouraged as you read this book. We hope you will be empowered by the many practical, reproducible, empirically based as well as common-knowledge *ideas for improving your church's ministry.* They will come in the form of guidelines and recommendations in the following chapters. You will find them identified at the beginning of each chapter, and all sixty of them appear in the Ideas for Improving Your Church's Ministry index at the end of the book. Also, at the end of each chapter you will find helpful questions for reflection and discussion, and suggestions for getting started.

Don't buy into the bogus sales pitch that it's all about more bodies, bucks, and buildings. Loren Mead, in *New Possibilities for Small Churches,* gave a perspective as true today as when it was written: "Small is enough. It is enough for keeping on. It is enough for faithfulness.... Small is enough for holding lives and families together and for making a contribution to a community. It is enough for breaking bread and sharing wine, for wrestling with the scriptures, for calling one another to new life. It is enough for praying, for following Jesus."[1]

Enough is enough! Not just enough to survive or to be good enough, but enough to be great. Small is enough and small is the future. In *Small, Strong Congregations,* Kennon Callahan makes a prediction based on his many fruitful years of helping countless small churches around the globe:

> The twenty-first century is the century of small, strong congregations. More people will be drawn to small, strong congregations than any other kind of congregation. Yes, there are many mega-congregations; their number is increasing greatly. Nevertheless, around the planet, the vast majority of congregations will be small and strong, and the vast majority of people will be in these congregations.[2]

Don't expect this book to just be a pep talk and a pat on the head. It's about power. Jesus said, "I will build my church" (Matthew 16:18). He also said, "Fear not, little flock, for it is your Father's good pleasure to give you the kingdom" (Luke 12:32, RSV). Jesus will build his church. He will empower you to be faithful in becoming all that he wants you to be. God takes pleasure in giving you all that you need to further his kingdom.

God loves small churches.

SECTION ONE
small by CHOICE

1
why SMALLER is better

---

ideas for IMPROVING your church's ministry

1. Four biblical applications to combat feelings of inadequacy
2. A biblical strategy for responding to God's leading
3. Ten vital qualities for identifying your church's strengths

---

Small churches often get a bad rap: "They are not reaching out to the community enough." "They are not offering enough programs to meet people's needs." "They're not growing fast enough." In short, they are not big enough.

Who are these seeming black sheep of the church? What do they look like? George Barna classifies small churches as those with fewer than 100 regular attenders. Barna's research reveals that small churches comprise one-half of all the Protestant churches in America. In *The Second Coming of the Church,* Barna paints a rather pathetic picture of the small church:

The small churches tend to offer a Sunday morning worship time, complete with organ and hymns; a Sunday evening service, attended by a handful of the faithful; and perhaps a midweek evening service, designed for in-depth Bible teaching. There is often a midweek daytime Bible study taught by the pastor and attended by a few of the older women in the body. Additional programs are limited in number and nature; those that exist reflect the advanced age of most members (for example, hospital visitation, bingo, women's service circle).[1]

We agree with Barna's observation that many, perhaps most, small churches are "involved in an unchanging set of programs and events designed to satisfy a well-defined, consistent group of needs relative to a rather circumscribed group of people."[2] One is led to assume that bigger is better—it must be! However, a quick look at what many, perhaps most, bigger churches look like is telling. Mid-sized and large churches are, according to Barna, hurting, too. The primary goals of large churches (1,000 or more members, comprising less than three percent of America's churches) tend to be more visitors, more money, and more programs. They tend to share the vision of something for everybody, defining success in terms of ever-increasing size, ever-expanding facilities, ever-broadening programs, ever-growing budgets—and in some cases an over-inflated image. Their common heartbeat seems to be: "We're meeting people's needs." Maybe they are. But are they transforming lives?

Barna's research revealed that most of those who "make a decision for Christ wander away from the church within eight weeks of making such a decision," mainly because no one disciples or mentors them.[3] They do not adequately learn the meaning or application of their new-found faith. Many therefore never become true converts. They may be "spiritually crippled for life," says Barna. He adds, "If the Church were more diligent about equipping people to understand their faith and to use their gifts and abilities to serve others, this would not happen with such horrific frequency."[4]

Bigger is not better if it makes it easier for people to church-hop just to spice up their lives; easier to avoid commitment and accountability; easier to resist interference with their lifestyles; easier to reposition Christianity as a commodity for consumption.

Over the past forty-two years, we have experienced all sizes and shapes of churches across a variety of denominations. Among the things we have learned is that a church ought not try to be all things to all people. As some advise, "Don't be a mile wide and an inch deep." A small church can be exactly what God called it to be and do very well.

Too many churches of all sizes have merely become spiritual pit stops rather than spiritual homes. Churches have become one-stop-shops for meeting all our personal needs. At their best, churches are places where we come first and foremost to know God, to love and learn to follow him. A small church is suited especially well for the role of spiritual home and for providing a healthy environment for intimacy with God, the Father. This is the first of several advantages of small churches discussed in this chapter.

God's Desire for Small Churches

Too many small churches fail to become the spiritual homes God wants them to be. They feel inadequate and make excuses, much as Moses did to avoid doing what God called him to do. Moses' experience, recorded in Exodus 3 and 4, is instructive when applied to the experience of these small churches.

First, Moses asks, "Who am I?" and God replies, "I will be with you." Many small churches feel woefully inadequate to do things anywhere nearly as well as larger and megachurches. They ask, "How can we do what you are calling us to do?" and God replies, "I will be with you."

Second, Moses asks, "What shall I tell them?" and God replies, "You shall say to the Israelites, 'I AM has sent me to you.' " The small church often gets off-message by trying to keep up with all the latest cultural changes, worship styles, and evangelism programs, and asks, "What should our message be?" God replies, "Tell them about me."

Third, Moses asks, "What if they do not believe me or listen to me?" and God replies, "What is that in your hand?" The small church, again feeling inadequate, too often believes that it cannot make a difference because it has insufficient financial and human resources. Too often, however, churches do not notice how God has already been working. They have overlooked the very real opportunities afforded by their location, the interests and skills of their people, or the exact nature of God's calling of them to ministry. So they ask, "What can we do to reach our community for Christ?" God replies, "You do not need to become something you are not. I have called you to what I want you to be. Look at what is already in your hand."

Fourth, Moses says, "I am not eloquent," and God replies, "I will help you speak and will teach you what to say." The small church usually has not thought seriously enough about its calling or the spiritual gifts of its members, and therefore says, "We do not have the right people to carry out all we have to do." God replies, "I will provide for all your needs."

A small church can take great comfort in applying what Moses learned: God will be with you; tell them about God; you do not need to become something you are not because God has called you to what he wants you to be; and God will provide for all your needs.

In fact, churches can respond to God's leading more quickly when they are smaller in size. They are not weighed down by bulky bureaucracies, ponderous planning processes, unwieldy budgets, and heavily funded programs. Healthy small churches are not bound by inertia. They are actively looking for where God is at work and are joining him.

We have been helped greatly by Henry Blackaby and Claude King, who have firmly focused our thoughts on the biblical truth that God is already and is always at work around us. In *Experiencing God,* Blackaby and King offer a remarkable biblical strategy they developed for looking to see where God is working and then joining him.[5]

God is asking small churches in America, "What do you have in your hand?" Every small church should ask itself why it must work so hard to get big and why it thinks that making itself bigger is the way to grow. God has made the small church what God wants it to be and eagerly desires that we who are already there would enter in. God is already at work all around and within us. Our job is to find out what God is doing and join him. That might mean sharing ministries with other churches based on effectiveness rather than fearfully protecting our church membership. It might mean supplying time and resources to plant a new church. Or it might mean seriously incorporating disciple-making into every area of the church's life. A healthy church can do these things and, as a result, grow in many different ways.

A healthy church will inevitably grow in some way. A growing church, however, is not necessarily healthy. The standard is not numbers, facilities, or programs. The standard is health! A healthy small church is free to look and see where God is working and then to come and join in God's work.

God's Design for Small Churches

Healthy small churches do not to have to become something they are not. In his *The Big Small Church Book,* David Ray warns that small churches "are the right size to be all that God calls a church to be. They are not premature, illegitimate, malnourished, or incomplete versions of 'real' churches."[6] The message is clear: Don't try to behave like the big church you are not. Be the small church God has called you to be.

Your small church is the right size and is in the right place to be faithful to your calling and fruitful in your ministry. In God's economy, no little places exist where God cannot accomplish great things. In their book, *No Little Places,* Ron

Klassen and John Koessler insist that "whatever your church's size, location, or circumstances, God can do great things there. Because with God, there are no little places."[7] They further state that to fulfill your small church's potential, you need not try to become a scaled-down version of a big church. Instead, your church can capitalize on its greatest strengths: intimacy and involvement. It is common knowledge that these two strengths are actual advantages of small churches when compared to large churches. Ray notes these similar advantages:[8]

- Intense caring for one another
- Experiential education style that leaves room for exploration
- Intimate, participatory worship
- Passionate outreach to a hurting world

We see some additional advantages:

- Having high expectations for membership, ministry in each one's area of giftedness, preparation for classes, and sharing one's faith
- Teaching people to live as disciples of Jesus rather than attracting them to superficial benefits of consumer Christianity
- Commitment to a corporate lifestyle based on biblical values
- Commitment to *conversion* growth, not transfer growth

Major study one: Cynthia Woolever and Deborah Bruce, in *Beyond the Ordinary,* report the strengths, or advantages of small churches, discovered through the rigor of scientific analysis. In the largest, most representative study ever conducted in the United States, they profiled more than 300,000 worshipers in over 2,000 churches. Their focus was on ten vital qualities of strong churches: (1) growing spiritually, (2) meaningful worship, (3) participation in the congregation, (4) having a sense of belonging, (5) caring for children and youth, (6) focusing on the community, (7) sharing faith, (8) welcoming new people, (9) empowering leadership, and (10) vision for the future.[9] Among other things, the study found:

- Six strengths (numbers 1, 3, 4, 5, 7 and 9) met statistical tests for significance, that is, they were too large to happen by chance. Small churches (fewer than 100 people) have the advantage in five of these six—growing spiritually, participating in the congregation, having a sense of belonging, sharing faith, and empowering leadership. Mid-sized churches of 100 to 350 have the advantage in the sixth—caring for children and youth. Large churches of more than 350 do not have the advantage in any of the six.[10]
- Three strengths (growing spiritually, having a sense of belonging, and empowering leadership) are key factors in *extraordinary* churches—and small churches have the advantage in all three![11]

Woolever and Bruce note that small churches come out on top of their composite Growing Spiritually Index, leading to one conclusion: "Small congregations tend to be spiritually stronger than other congregations. In this area of congregational life (spiritual growth), small congregations have an advantage. Pound for pound, small congregations carry a lot of spiritual weight!"[12]

The activities described within the five statistically significant strength categories that favor small churches are worthy of note. Activities wherein small churches excel are:

- Private devotions (at least a few times weekly)
- Bible study
- Prayer ministry
- Small groups
- Giving (at least 5 percent or more of net income)
- Assuming leadership positions
- Participating in decision making
- Inviting others (who are not members elsewhere) to worship
- Seeking opportunities to talk about faith
- Participating in outreach ministries
- Pastor encourages people to find and use their spiritual gifts
- Pastor takes into account the ideas of others[13]

Small-church advantages. Size matters! In Section Two, we will clarify and expand on all the advantages we have listed so far. These advantages are God's design for the healthy small church, which has the following characteristics:

1. Pastoral leadership is faithful to the biblical model.
   - Everyone is a minister.
   - The appeal of size, power, and influence is resisted.
2. Being a church family is a reality.
   - Everyone is included.
   - Church gatherings are communal as well as relational.
3. Members live in covenant with one another.
   - They focus on disciple-making, mutual accountability, solemn commitment to the body of Christ, and a strong sense of belonging in God's family.
   - Church governance is free from politics.
4. Everyone's spiritual gifts are used in ministry.
5. Christian education is viewed as a means for people to become apprentices to Jesus to live out Christ's kingdom imperatives.
   - Education takes place within a family context rather than creating separate generational cultures.
6. The congregation is free to be innovative in worship.
   - Worship is truly participatory and genuinely communal. → *prayer concerns*
7. Prayer is foundational for everything the church does.
   - The church is a house of prayer, with corporate prayer as the cornerstone.
8. Stewardship structures eliminate the pressure to give but encourage the pleasure of giving.
   - The church also adjusts its corporate lifestyle to become a biblically faithful, giving community.
9. A Spirit-formed church is coming into being.
   - As the congregation abides in the Holy Spirit, his presence and power pervade the life of the church.
10. Relationship evangelism and church multiplication become part of the corporate DNA.

In Their Own Words

We recently conducted a survey of the small churches in our denomination and asked the pastors to tell us about the advantages of being small. The following responses express quite well many of the advantages we have found:

"I get so excited telling other pastors and friends about being blessed to pastor a church where the people are growing in their walk with the Lord and have a desire to be the church God wants them to be! It is exciting to be the pastor of the church where the people want me to do the biblically described work of equipping them and where they want to be the ministers. It is a great blessing to see the degree of maturity and commitment that exists [in] this small group of believers." *Franklin Missionary Church, Franklin, Nebraska*

"I love it when we help someone heal from any kind of hurt. I love our commitment to missions. I love our financial freedom. I love it when we can talk without fear of offense or anger. I love it that we are a family and not just a congregation." *West York Missionary Church, York, Pennsylvania*

"We are relationship-based rather than program-based. We are more like a family than a well-oiled machine. Families that attended other churches sporadically or not at all prior to coming to our little church are now not only attending regularly but participating, giving, and inviting others." *Celebrate Life Christian Fellowship, Bryan, Ohio*

 "The people of our church are being trained to understand that ministry will only happen when they use their spiritual gifts to lead in a ministry that God lays on their hearts. We want to be ministry-driven, not program-support driven." *Potsdam Missionary Church, Potsdam, Ohio*

"We long to be a New Testament church. We try to practice an interactive learning experience in a contemporary and
relaxed environment. People always comment about the sense
of love and acceptance they feel and the impact that learning
with us has on their lives. Many small churches try to run a
typical ministry on a smaller scale. We seek to know what
God calls us to do and then do it with all our might." *Lake
Missionary Church, Angola, Indiana*

For Reflection and Discussion

1. The pastors of small churches who were quoted are excited about their churches' ministries. What did you sense in
   your spirit when you read their comments? *energy*
2. One could conclude that being small is a virtue in itself
   and use it to maintain the status quo. Why is this a wrong
   conclusion?
3. People and pastors often apologize for being small, as
   though they have not grown as fast as they should or they
   lack the resources to make a difference. What would you
   say to someone who obviously feels that small is inferior?
4. What is your first impression of how your church com-
   pares to the ten characteristics of strong churches?
5. Keeping in mind the stated principles of the exchange
   between God and Moses, take an inventory of your
   church by answering these questions:
   - What are some instances when you knew God was
     with you and your church?
   - What ways and methods has your church used to tell
     others about God?
   - What size, shape, or strategy have you been tempted to
     use that is not really you?
   - Is there a unique niche it seems God wants your church
     to fill? What is it?

- How has God already provided generously for the needs of your church?

Getting Started

1. After completing your inventory in question five above, gather as much information as you can about a specific ministry niche you think you might have been given to fill.
   - How is God already at work in this area?
   - What new approaches might God want you to try?
   - What resources do you feel are lacking?
   - What things do you need to avoid in being faithful in this area of ministry?
2. Organize a time (an evening?) of celebration of what God is doing in your church. Include singing and testimonies of people whose lives have been changed because of your church's ministries. List the areas mentioned in this chapter where small churches have been particularly successful, and invite people to testify to instances in areas where the research has confirmed what they have experienced.

2

taking your church's PULSE

---

ideas for IMPROVING your church's ministry

4. Eight essential qualities for measuring your church's health
5. Ten warning signs for assessing whether your church is becoming unhealthy

---

The church, in general, is sick. George Barna states bluntly in *The Second Coming of the Church:*

> Most Christians ... have fallen prey to the same disease as their worldly counterparts. We think and behave no differently from anyone else. This problem is compounded by the fact that the individuals in positions of Christian leadership generally do an inadequate job of leading God's people. The systems, structures, institutions, and relational networks developed for the furtherance of the Church are archaic, inefficient, and ineffective—and, perhaps, even unbiblical.[1]

If the people themselves as well as the leadership and organizational structures are all part of the problem, what can be done about it? Where does one begin? A healthy church consists of healthy people. Therefore, we can gauge the spiritual health of a church by taking a look at what people in it, including the pastor, are doing. What are they doing to grow in their knowledge of the Lord, to rekindle their passion for the Lord, to minister to one another, and to reach the lost for Christ?

Good prayer!

This idea is not new. It is very similar to a prayer Richard of Chichester wrote in the thirteenth century containing the words, "O, dear Lord, three things I pray: To see Thee more clearly, love Thee more dearly, follow Thee more nearly."[2] These words promote a vision of reaching up to God, the Father Almighty, to see him unmistakably, to love him passionately, and to take his hand and follow him faithfully wherever he leads.

Reaching up to God is a picture of health! Psalm 36:9 says, "For with you is the fountain of life; in your light we see light" (NIV). All life proceeds from and is sustained by the Creator, and only through the Lord can it be perfected. The church, however, has a strong tendency to try to heal itself by reaching out before reaching up. It tries to breathe new life into itself by finding new ways to grow in size and in its outreach. Such an approach puts the proverbial cart before the horse! Is it possible that this actually fosters the disease Barna warns us about?

Nothing will get a church healthy faster than realigning its heart upward and rekindling its passion for God. Then God releases power through the church and redirects its efforts to accomplish God's purposes. Everyone ought to feel the pulse of such a church, where the people say, "God is working through us." We have heard them say it. God releasing power and revealing his presence to and through a healthy church is such a contrast to churches dominated by the failures of human politics and pressures to succeed!

Our vision for the healthy small church is people saying, "We know the Lord, we love the Lord, and the Lord is working through us." We see people intentionally and enthusiastically learning who God is, creating the context for God to work through us by loving him, and launching ministries that release God's power. We see it in our own small church.

The Gathering Church

We started a church in the summer of 1995. No fanfare or impressive launch accompanied the startup—it sort of happened over time. We had attended a number of different churches over several years and had not found them, in general, to be either intellectually challenging or spiritually invigorating. Many of the churches, we felt, had fallen asleep at the switch. They were attracting believers who seemed to be seeking emotional security, doctrinal comfort, and personal fulfillment. These churches were not, however, moving people beyond their own personal cravings and desires. They were not teaching those who had received the gift of grace a more comprehensive knowledge of the Giver. They were not worshiping the God they personally experienced and loved as much as the God they learned about through the biblical record of his activity throughout history. In other words, they were not praising God for who he is as much as for what he has done. Finally, they were praying more for their own purposes—to receive God's blessings for themselves—than for releasing God's power to achieve his purposes.

During that period of time, I (Rosie) led a number of Bible studies. Men and women participated who were not active in any church, as did many who were attending churches in the area. The church-goers came because they were not learning and growing deeper in their faith. Many were biblically illiterate; some knew very little about the fundamentals of Christianity, even though they had been members of evangelical churches for many years. Some church-goers were not believers. God used those Bible studies both to teach and to lead people to Christ. He also gave to several people the desire to gather together regularly for prayer, study, and worship.

Out of this, The Gathering Church was born. God encouraged us from the very beginning. The teachers he blessed us with were evidence he was working in our midst. We joined God in making Christian education central to our vision. We also were led to focus on church dropouts (including those who have been hurt by their churches) and nonbelievers. God brought us several church dropouts who intensely disliked sermons. To them, sermons ranged from the vacuous and "dumbed down" to culture-driven "psychobabble." We learned that we could worship without a sermon and implemented the biblical guidelines for giving everyone an opportunity to contribute.[3] What a way to worship God—as participants, not spectators!

We learned to eliminate politics and pressure from the areas of governing and giving. These were two other major complaints we encountered from the large number of Christians living in our area who had quit attending church. First, we found a way to allow the Holy Spirit to select—rather than our electing—those who served as leaders. As a result, people were no longer hesitant to serve, and the competitive sense of "I won" or "I lost" was removed. Also, it has added a strong feeling that God knows what the demands on each person will be in the future and is choosing the right combination of people for the tasks that lie ahead.

Second, we discovered that the Holy Spirit is entirely capable of bringing in the money we need and of selecting and directing where the money should go. No fundraisers, no pledges, no passing the plate, and no manipulative sermons. Seeing God working through us, in God's way, and in God's time, has given us true joy!

Does all this sound radical? Our procedures for facilitating the activity of the Holy Spirit in worship, leadership, and finances indeed are a radical departure from the status quo. Later we will share these procedures along with the many other things we have discovered while "doing church." We are not saying that what we have discovered is the only way or even the best way. We are saying, however, that a small church has significant advantages in creating an environment for releasing God's presence and power through his people. And if God is at the helm, it will be a healthy church.

A healthy small church will feature the advantages we listed in Chapter 1. In this chapter, we focus on the fundamental ingredients that make for a healthy church.

Faithfulness

God has a bias for smallness. In *The Big Small Church Book*, David Ray states, "Part of God's bias for the small is a result of the temptation for the big to believe they are the masters of their own destiny and to become a god unto themselves. The small, with no alternative, must rely on God's grace rather than their own clout."[4] Jesus commends the church in Philadelphia for its faithfulness while having "little power." Revelation 3:8 in the Amplified Bible says, "I know your [record of] works *and* what you are doing. See! I have set before you a door wide open, which no one is able to shut; I know that you have little power, and yet you have kept my Word *and* guarded my message, and have not renounced *or* denied my name."

What a picture that is—Jesus' gracious gift of a guaranteed future for evangelism and spiritual usefulness! The church is weak: small in numbers, poor in worldly goods, of little account in the eyes of the modern world, yet it is resting in the strength of the Almighty to be faithful in all things in order to further the kingdom of God. Again, the small church has the advantage.

Contrast this picture with that of the polar opposite of the small church—the megachurch. Os Guinness, in *Dining with the Devil*, sees megachurches as dining with the devil of modernity:

The megachurches are a gigantic mutation in the churches' age-old "edifice complex." They are the natural counterparts of megamalls, super-supermarkets, and multiplex cinemas, and resemble a cross between shopping malls and theme parks—modernity's ultimate in people-moving selling-machines. The result is "spiritual emporiums" or the "malling of religion"—grand cathedrals of consumption, one-stop church complexes ... with multiple-option boutiques catering to diverse needs.[5]

Certainly not all megachurches uncritically capitulate to the dangers of modernity. Nevertheless, we must heed the warning. Ultimately, Guinness warns, super-sized churches end up molding and marketing the biblical message to their constituents' needs and their own insatiable need for growth, thereby substituting numerical forcefulness for biblical faithfulness. It is not a pretty picture:

> Gone are the hard sayings of Jesus.... With all its need-meeting emphasis, there is little ... that stands crosswise to the world. Messianic marketing is [creating churches holding to a theology] criticized earlier by Richard Niebuhr as 'a God without wrath [bringing] men without sin into a Kingdom without judgement through the ministrations of a Christ without a Cross.'[6]

David Ray notes how Scripture consistently "affirms the few, the small, and the insignificant who live by faithfulness rather than forcefulness. With few exceptions, biblical faithfulness does not come from, or result in, large numbers."[7] Nor does biblical greatness come from large numbers. Rather, greatness is a product of faithfulness. God chooses "those who are powerless" and "things despised by the world, things counted as nothing at all" to accomplish great things (1 Corinthians 1:26-29).

Regardless of size or clout, those faithful churches through whom God accomplishes great things achieve an element of greatness for themselves, as when someone says, "That's a great church!" Big or small. However, God receives *all* the glory when something great is born out of a church that is faithful, small, and seemingly insignificant.

God delights to bless those who make the kingdom of God their primary concern (Luke 12:31). The Lord wants to give you the kingdom. In your weakness, depend on God and you will inherit the kingdom of God (2 Corinthians 12:9). Don't be afraid, faithful—great—little flock.

Fruitfulness

Faithfulness is one vital sign that a church is alive and well. Fruitfulness is the other. Perhaps we could measure the vitality of a church by the sum total of its faithfulness and fruitfulness: how much of God's purpose and presence go in plus how much of God's love and ministry come out. Or perhaps we should look at it as we do a tree and its fruit: "A healthy tree produces good fruit, and an unhealthy tree produces bad fruit" (Matthew 7:17). In other words, a healthy church produces good fruit. Faithfulness to biblically life-transforming activities (see Section Two) produces a healthy church. And a healthy church produces fruit.

Major study two: The best measure we have found for assessing the fruitfulness of a church comes from Christian Schwarz's eight essential qualities of healthy churches, found in his book, *Natural Church Development.* Schwarz conducted the most comprehensive study ever done on church health, involving more than 1,000 churches in thirty-two countries on five continents.

One of Schwarz's many interesting conclusions is that, of the eight essential qualities of a healthy church, "gift-oriented ministry" is the key indicator of church health.[8] In a recent interview in *Leadership* magazine, Schwarz stated that as a church grows in size, its health declines. The reason, according to his findings, lies in the percentage of people who exercise their spiritual gifts in ministry. He observes, "In churches with [fewer] than 100 in attendance, it's 31 percent. You can say that's not much. But if you compare that with churches of over 1,000 in attendance, which average only 17 percent, you see there is a decline in quality [or health]."[9]

Considering Schwarz's data, small churches clearly have the advantage with regard to church health. The clincher came when Schwarz looked at the entire basket of fruit: (1) empowering leadership, (2) gift-oriented ministry, (3) passionate spirituality, (4) functional structures, (5) inspiring worship service, (6) holistic small groups, (7) need-oriented evangelism, and (8) loving relationships. He found that small churches outperformed bigger churches in all but one: inspiring worship service.

Unhealthy churches. This is all well and good for those of us committed to small churches, but we must not take church health for granted. At The Gathering, we evaluate ourselves each year on the eight essential qualities of a healthy church. (See the Appendix for the questions we discuss.) We work to improve our apparent weakest quality or qualities and to track our year-by-year growth as a healthy church.

We also are continuously aware of our faithfulness to the ten life-transforming activities (Section 2) that produce a healthy church, and can readily pick up any early signs of being on the road to becoming unhealthy. An unhealthy church might be defined as a church without joy that has not served the Lord with enthusiasm for the abundant benefits that have been received, a church that does not rejoice in all that is being accomplished because of the Lord's blessings (Deuteronomy 28:47; cf. Deuteronomy 12:7).

The following are important warning signs of an unhealthy church:
1. Relationships are dominated by church politics.
2. Leaders are accountable only to themselves and to their own agendas.
3. Women and/or children are treated as second-class citizens.
4. Low expectations of leaders and members limit opportunities for seeing God at work.
5. People participate in ministry only when assigned to fill vacancies and when it is convenient.

6. Evangelism is seen by each member as someone else's job.
7. Giving to ministries outside the church is held hostage to meeting operating needs within the church.
8. Worship is focused on entertaining and meeting the needs of the people.
9. The sermon is the primary method for teaching the Word of God and for making disciples.
10. Corporate prayer is rare.

The Future

We have been looking at the *vitality* of a healthy church, but what is the *vision* of a healthy church? In the previously cited *Leadership* interview, Schwarz was asked the final question, "You champion smaller churches. What is their role in the near future?" He responded:

Up to now most church growth writing uses examples from big churches. Even if authors don't intend to set a big church as the goal, people get that impression because all the examples are from big churches. Ninety-five percent of the literature on church growth and health should concentrate on healthy, small churches that can multiply and give birth to other small churches. The importance of celebrating small churches and aiming to multiply small churches is strategic. And it will increase.[10]

The Gathering's vision is to be strategic rather than settled into a typical ministry on a smaller scale. Our vision from the very beginning has been to remain a small church and to intentionally spin off numerical growth and contribute resources for strategically located new church plants. The Gathering is small not because of fatalistic resignation or demographic default, but because of kingdom-oriented choice. We are devoted to seeing disciples making disciples, to raising up workers from the harvest for the harvest. We are strategically involved in small churches planting small churches.

Does your church have a similar vision? Maybe as the pastor, you would love to implement new ideas, but feel your church is settled and not about to change. Perhaps you feel like a pastor friend of ours who said recently, "All I do is manage debt and cater to the whims of the people." Do you feel that the heart of God is not beating within the church you serve?

The primary task of your spiritual leadership in the corporate change process is calling people themselves to change, not just to accept changes without their involvement. The fundamental goal we must keep in mind is not to move people through a time of transition of implementing changes, but to move people through a faithful journey of personal transformation. Our job as pastors is to awaken in the people of God an expectation and awareness of God's presence pulsating throughout the entire church—her polity, her programs, and her people—in fruitful ministry to further God's kingdom.

For Reflection and Discussion

1. How do you see the Lord working through the people in your church?
2. How would you rate your church on the eight essential qualities of healthy churches?
3. What would you expect to see in a healthy small church that utilizes the spiritual gifts of its people? (Thinking about how a family functions might help.)
4. Which of the warning signs of an unhealthy church do you think might apply to your church? Why do you think this?
5. Proverbs 29:18 says, "Where there is no vision, the people perish." What vision does your church have? Is it "disciples making disciples" and "churches planting churches," or is it "us four and no more" or is it something else?

Getting Started

1. Urge the leaders of your church to take your church's pulse using the "Essential Qualities of a Healthy Church" questions found in the Appendix. They could discuss the agreed-upon weakest area and devise an action plan: What changes could be made? Who will implement them? By when?
2. After completing question four above, write a prescription to make your church "better."
3. Envision a time when your church might be involved in planting another church. Describe what the new church would be like, even though its location might be much different from yours. Give the church plant a name that represents your vision for a healthy church.

making your small church GREAT

3

shepherding

---

ideas for IMPROVING your church's ministry

I (Rosie) like my sheep. I have always said, "If you don't like sheep, you shouldn't be a shepherd." Sheep have a mind of their own. They do not always want to do what you know is best for them. They butt heads to gain supremacy. They have been known to injure the shepherd. They get sick at inconvenient times. Yet, if you like sheep, all of these behaviors are just temporary inconveniences.

We have raised four-legged sheep for more than twenty years. They daily remind us of what God means by saying we are the sheep of his pasture. We have learned what it means to tend the flock and to have a shepherd's heart. Shepherding has taken on a rich meaning for us, in total agreement with the biblical description of shepherding, which includes knowing the

cute but true

state of your flock and putting your heart into its care (Proverbs 27:23).

Shepherding is first on our list of the ten biblically life-transforming activities that produce healthy churches. We believe it is vital for small churches to honor the biblical concept of pastoral leadership. We also believe that small churches have the advantage in being faithful to the biblical model, refusing to keep ministry from the people and resisting the appeal of size, power, and influence.

Knowing the State of the Sheep

Some churches, unfortunately, do not know how to care for sheep properly. Their shepherds practice poor pasture management. That is, they put all their sheep into one big pasture and just leave them there. In time, of course, the grass is eaten down and there is no more nourishment for the sheep. So the sheep complain. They *loudly* complain. Meanwhile, the shepherds cast about for other sources of food for their sheep to make them happy and quiet them down.

What these shepherds should be doing instead is dividing their pasture into smaller pastures and rotating their flock through them. The condition of the grass helps determine how long the sheep may stay in one location and where they are moved next. Using this method, the grass where they are is never too short. (Overgrazing will kill the grass and even give the sheep worms.) Shepherds who truly know the state of their sheep practice good pasture management.

Knowing the state of the sheep essentially involves first knowing their needs for nourishment, then their giftedness for ministry, and finally, their reasons for separating themselves from the flock. The question the shepherd must ask, first and foremost, is, Are they getting the nourishment they need? Without good pasture, the sheep will not flourish. Many churches go wrong precisely on this point. Consider, for example, churches where people are drawn to the Sunday service as the showcase and place to be fed, the big pasture where they graze. The majority of people do not move to other pastures within the church for nourishment. They just keep overgrazing the same old grass until they begin to realize they're no longer being fed. Then they start complaining. They complain loudly: "We're not being fed! We're tired of the same old sermons. We're bored." (They have spiritual worms, so to speak.)

Sunday service is not the only or even the best place for teaching the flock. To answer the question "Are they being fed?" requires that sheep find nourishment in many different pastures. The shepherd needs to know something about each sheep:

- Is he reading his Bible daily?
- Is she keeping the membership covenant?
- Is he involved in an area of ministry for which he is gifted?
- What class might she need to take next?
- Is he attending worship regularly?
- Does she participate in corporate prayer?
- Does he need to be in a small group?

Second, the shepherd does well to consider how the sheep are individually gifted. Unfortunately, involvement in local church ministry usually works like this: Need ushers? Need choir members? Need nursery workers? Need Sunday school teachers? Put a notice in the Sunday bulletin asking for volunteers: "Anyone interested?" This is not good shepherding. A good shepherd knows his sheep. He knows that the sheep need to be rotated through different sections of pasture because they need different kinds and quantities of nourishment. Good shepherding means knowing that if people need different pastures, the shepherd's business is to know their gifts as well as their needs, and not to ask for volunteers.

Good shepherding also means knowing that a mature ewe will not go through an open gate if fresh hay is in the manger. In other words, if the pasture is always fresh, people will not leave to go to other churches.

Third, the shepherd needs to know whether the sheep are okay. An old proverb reads, "The health of the flock is in the eye of the shepherd." This means that the shepherd keeps a watchful eye over her sheep at all times. She knows her sheep so well that she senses when something is not right. She can walk into the barn or out into a pasture and sense that something is wrong. Maybe she smells a bad odor, indicating foot rot or that the sheep got into something they should not have. Or perhaps the ears of a sheep are lowered and it is listless, indicating that it is sick. Maybe one of the sheep is not chewing its cud or is grinding its teeth, indicating intense concentration on something wrong internally. Or, when the shepherd walks out to one of her pastures, she sees the sheep all lined up staring off in the same direction. Something is out there, perhaps a dog or coyote. The same sort of thing is in evidence when we walk through the door of an unhealthy church. There is a hush; disengaged fear hangs in the air. Something is wrong.

The health and safety of a flock of sheep correspond in several ways to healthy and unhealthy churches. We have noticed that when a sheep separates itself from the flock, other than when it is lost, it does so for a reason. If it is a ewe that will be lambing soon, going off alone is the natural thing to do. However, if any other sheep is separating itself from the flock, not wanting to have anything to do with the other sheep, that sheep is sick.

The same thing happens in unhealthy churches. People who quit attending church and do not seem to want to have anything to do with other believers are spiritually sick. Unfortunately, they are often forgotten. We have heard many such folks complain bitterly that no one from their former church contacted them at any time to ask how they were doing and if everything was all right, much less to tell them they were missed. By contrast, the shepherd of a healthy church searches for sheep who stray away and attempts to bring them safely home again (Ezekiel 34:16).

Another thing we have noticed is that sheep sometimes get bloated when they are moved from a sparse pasture to a lush one and allowed to eat to their heart's content. They get sick from eating too much rich grass. They need a steady diet instead. All or none, feast or famine, is the pattern in unhealthy churches where the learning environment is poor. Little good teaching takes place, and to fill the void and keep people from complaining, the church holds occasional special events. Here come the dynamic speakers, life-changing seminars, and popular video series. They hype it to the hilt and drop the whole load all at once. It is exciting, but how many people can take it all in? How many people can fully digest all they do take in? In contrast to the event mentality, a healthy church offers a steady diet of ongoing, multiple learning opportunities to help the body of believers grow to maturity in Christ. Avoid the event mentality that bloats the sheep and covers up a poor learning environment.

The Heart of the Shepherd

Knowing the state of the sheep is an expression of the heart. This, more than anything else, distinguishes the good shepherd from every other type of leader. The most compelling example of a shepherd's heart that I (Kirk) have ever seen took place many years ago in the little stand-alone garage on our property when we were living in Illinois.

It was in the dead of winter, the temperature near zero degrees, around midnight. Rosie was sitting on the dirt floor in a small enclosure surrounded by several stacked bales of straw. The only heat came from a heat lamp we had removed from the chicken house. Cradled in her arms was a newborn lamb, which Rosie had helped the struggling ewe deliver just moments earlier. The little lamb was weak and unable to nurse. His life was in danger.

Rosie the shepherd prayed to Jesus the Shepherd. She prayed for the life of that little lamb and asked for guidance in getting him to begin nursing. Her prayer was being answered as she got up and went into the house to put together a mixture of evaporated milk and honey. As she heated it up on the stove, she had no idea that (as she found out later) it was the perfect mixture of ingredients the lamb needed to get into his system.

Armed with an eyedropper filled with the warm liquid, the shepherd returned to the barn and began dripping the milk and honey into the lamb's mouth. The problem was, however, that most of the liquid was sliding out of one corner of the lamb's mouth. He simply did not have the strength to suckle properly. Then God provided a very unlikely resource: a cat! Our cat just "happened" to be in the area on that cold and wintry evening and just "happened" to jump up onto Rosie's lap and began licking the milky liquid off the corner of the lamb's mouth. As the cat licked, the lamb's mouth was stimulated to begin moving and, miraculously, the lamb began to drink. I kept the mixture heating on the stove at just the right temperature, running back and forth between the house and garage with renewed supplies, while the lamb kept drinking and getting stronger. Rosie stayed out there all night, and by the next day the ewe was nursing her newborn lamb.

Our lamb story reveals that there is something special in the heart of a shepherd, a special kind of compassion and commitment. It reveals that the shepherd also has a Shepherd and is him- or herself, a sheep.[1]

The Good Shepherd

All sheep in every flock and all shepherds have one and the same Shepherd: the provider, director, protector. David, who was a shepherd, proclaimed, "The LORD is my shepherd, I shall not want" (Psalm 23:1, NASB). The Lord feeds, guides, and shields the sheep, and the sheep have everything they need.

God's provision for his sheep is for them to have all they need, to be complete in Jesus, the Good Shepherd. Jesus succinctly says, "I am the good Shepherd; I know my sheep and my sheep know me—just as the Father knows me and I know the Father—and I lay down my life for the sheep" (John 10:14-15, NIV).

Pastors obviously are undershepherds serving under the authority and mandate of the Good Shepherd. Jesus said to Peter, "Feed my sheep" (John 21:17). Peter passed that charge on to other pastoral leaders: "Feed the flock of God" (1 Peter 5:2, KJV). Paul, too, said in his farewell to the pastoral leadership of the church at Ephesus: "Feed the church of God" (Acts 20:28, KJV).

The biblical model for pastors is clearly this: Be a shepherd and love the Shepherd. Loving the Shepherd is the wellspring for loving the sheep. This is such an important truth. Love is the crowning virtue of the Good Shepherd and therefore it becomes the crowning excellence of his undershepherds as well.

In *The Minister as Shepherd*, Charles Jefferson writes:

Would you know, then, the work of a shepherd? Look at Jesus of Nazareth, that great Shepherd of the sheep, who stands before us forever the perfect pattern of [a good shepherd], the flawless example for all who are entrusted with the care of souls. 'I am the Good Pastor,' he says, 'I watch, I guard, I guide, I heal, I rescue, I feed. I love from the beginning, and I love to the end. Follow me!'[2]

Caring for the Sheep
Business Model versus Biblical Model

We are very much concerned that the Church has strayed from the biblical model and from the great Good Shepherd. The Church has gotten off track and off message. Pastors have developed a full-blown identity crisis. Many sheep are without a shepherd.

Glenn Wagner, in *Escape from Church, Inc.*, laments the corporate mentality takeover of the Church, with the devastating effects of sheep being without a shepherd and of pastoral leadership lacking the heart of a shepherd.

> I'm concerned about the growing numbers of "dropout Christians" who have been hurt and abused in churches that seem to see people as objects to be used for some grander scheme. I'm concerned about our high rate of pastoral burnout and the numbers of pastors being dismissed because they don't fit the corporate model now in vogue.[3]

The corporate, or business, model Wagner is talking about contrasts starkly with the covenant community, or biblical, model. Differences include:[4]

- Programs vs. people
- Money vs. ministry
- Entitlement vs. encouragement
- Competition vs. compassion
- Performance vs. process
- Numbers vs. nourishment
- Organization vs. organism

Through a series of articles patterned after the letters to the seven churches in the Book of Revelation, *Christianity Today* has described the degeneration of the Church. The articles were letters Jesus might write to churches today. The first was Eugene Peterson's "To the Suburban Church of North America," where he laid it out this way:

> I have this against you: you're far too impressed with Size

and Power and Influence. You are impatient with the small and the slow. You exercise little discernment between the ways of the world and my ways. It distresses me that you so uncritically copy the attitudes and methods that make your life in suburbia work so well. You grab onto anything that works and looks good. You do so many good things, but too often you do them in the world's way instead of mine, and so seriously compromise your obedience.[5]

By contrast, Susan Bauer's letter, "To the Rural Church," was much more affirming:

I know where you live: in a nation ruled by the god of Business.... Instead of a business, you rural churches have been a faithful family. You have refused to be professionalized; you have rejected the model of corporate effectiveness. Like me, you have chosen to be inefficient. You have lavished love and energy on the old and sick, on the isolated, on the very young. You have patiently waited decades for fruit. You ministers who spend your lives in the service of a congregation of thirty, you teachers who pour out your souls for a Bible class of five: you have understood what it means to be children of the Father and brothers and sisters of the Son.

You have also rejected those who claim to act in my name: those church-planting experts who advise that my people "target" only densely populated areas so that the largest number of people can be efficiently herded into the kingdom; the denominational leaders who have seen you as a useful training ground for inexperienced pastors who will soon move on to "better pulpits" in more worthy (and populated) places. You have endured this, and remained strong, and understood the truth: that size and efficiency are important only in the economy of hell.[6]

Both letters highlight the temptations of size, power, influence, and business—in Bauer's words, "important only in the economy of hell." When the biblical model is not followed, the most obvious effect on pastors is confusion regarding their pastoral role. Two wildly out-of-control forces fuel their confusion, discouragement, and burnout: the professionalization of pastoral ministry and secularization of church culture. These are not recent phenomena, and the pastoral identity crisis is nothing new.

Professionalization and Secularization

Twenty years ago, John Piper, in his essay "Brothers, We Are Not Professionals," made this plea for the deliverance of pastors from professionalism and "professionalizers":

> We pastors are being killed by the professionalizing of the pastoral ministry.... Professionalism has nothing to do with the essence and heart of the Christian ministry.... Banish professionalism from our midst, O God, and in its place put passionate prayer, poverty of spirit, hunger for God, rigorous study of holy things, white-hot devotion to Jesus Christ, utter indifference to all material gain, and unremitting labor to rescue the perishing, perfect the saints and glorify our sovereign Lord.[7]

What a passionate plea coming from a pastor with a true shepherd's heart!

Secularization of the church culture is the ongoing, unrelenting creation of a corporate reality driven by passion for the kinds of priorities listed earlier: programs, money, entitlement, competition, performance, numbers, and organization. It is the progressive enslavement to corporate effectiveness and the god of business. Secularization forces the pastor into a CEO mentality. The leader of a business is a CEO, so that is what the pastor must become.

However, since CEOs are business professionals and shepherds are not, undershepherds who are being pressured by their churches to be "CEO shepherds" must refuse.

They must reject the CEO mentality that says: "Do what a CEO would do." Rather, they must live as Jesus lived and provide proper food for the sheep, know the health of the sheep, and guide the sheep, all the while loving from beginning to end.

Equipping for Ministry

Caring for the sheep essentially involves (1) feeding the sheep, (2) equipping the sheep, and (3) watching over the sheep. Equipping is arguably the most fundamental principle of pastoral leadership. Paul tells us that the risen, triumphant Christ gave to his church the gift of undershepherds for the purpose of equipping the sheep for their work of ministry. "His intention was the perfecting *and* the full equipping of the saints (his consecrated people), [that they should do] the work of ministering toward building up Christ's body (the church)" (Ephesians 4:12, Amplified).

It follows that pastors should not do the work that God has given others in the body to do. Whenever they do so, they steal the blessings that belong to the other person. This deprives the whole body of the benefits the other person could have provided, and it fails to train him or her for doing ministry.

This reminds me (Rosie) of the difference between my winter sheep and my spring sheep. We don't actually have two flocks, but if you were to observe how they behave, you might think we did. I remove the sheep from the pasture in the winter, because grass does not grow well in Washington during the winter months. I keep them in the barn and exercise pen, where I supply them with plenty of fresh water and the right amount of hay twice a day. I also have to clean up after them, put down fresh bedding, and be present during lambing time. While winter sheep require a lot more work than during the other seasons, they also are a lot easier to manage. At the same time, keeping them in confined quarters is stifling to the sheep. They prefer open space within boundaries.

What do winter sheep have to do? Not much. They get up from time to time to drink out of the water bucket or eat some hay out of the manger. For some of them, the most exercise they get is shoving other sheep away from the hay. Pretty boring.

Spring sheep are different. Even old sedate ewes run and kick up their heels when they are taken to a fresh pasture. They feed themselves all day long, resting just long enough to chew on what they have eaten. They teach their young lambs how to feed themselves. The spring sheep are a shepherd's delight.

My spring sheep have taught me that the shepherd's job is to lead the sheep to fresh pasture. Once there, however, the sheep feed themselves, only occasionally needing direct help from the shepherd. I wonder how many pastors have missed that. How many pastors are maintaining their flock in winter quarters—on a permanent basis—boring their sheep and not permitting them to do what they are able to do? How many pastors are entertaining but not equipping their people? How many pastors are not allowing others to do the work that God has given them to do or, worse yet, doing it *for* them and thereby stealing their blessings?

Trampling the Pasture

Poor pastoral performance takes many forms: (1) managing the pasture poorly, (2) preempting others' blessings, (3) wintering sheep permanently, and also (4) trampling the pasture. Ezekiel cried out,

> "As for you, my flock, this is what the Sovereign LORD says
> .... Is it not enough for you to feed on the good pasture?
> Must you also trample the rest of your pasture with your
> feet? Is it not enough for you to drink clear water? Must you
> also muddy the rest with your feet? Must my flock feed on

what you have trampled and drink what you have muddied with your feet?" (Ezekiel 34:17-19, NIV).

Jeremiah records similar thoughts: "'Many shepherds will ruin my vineyard and trample down my field; they will turn my pleasant field into a desolate wasteland'" (Jeremiah 12:10, NIV).

Some readers might question whether Ezekiel is addressing shepherds as well as sheep. But we must remember that shepherds are also sheep. (When we forget that, it is that much easier to put pastors on a pedestal.) So we are talking about hirelings and false shepherds, as well as the flock of sheep. Turning to the New Testament, where Jesus exposes pharisaical attitudes, is instructive. Jesus also exposes undershepherds who trample the grass and muddy the water for God's sheep:

Then Jesus said to the crowds and to his disciples, "The teachers of religious law and the Pharisees are the official interpreters of the Scriptures. So practice and obey whatever they say to you, but don't follow their example. For they don't practice what they teach. They crush you with impossible religious demands and never lift a finger to help ease the burden…. How terrible it will be for you teachers of religious law and you Pharisees. Hypocrites! For you won't let others enter the Kingdom of Heaven, and you won't go in yourselves" (Matthew 23:1-4,13).

"They don't practice what they teach!" "They crush you with impossible religious demands!" "They won't let you enter the Kingdom of Heaven!" This sounds like spiritual abuse, pure and simple. As I (Kirk) point out in my book *Wounded Workers,* it is characteristic of spiritually abusive organizations.[8] These are pastors who use their position to require others to keep onerous rules and to live up to spiritual standards that they themselves never intended to observe.

These pastors muddy with their feet the water the sheep drink by substituting self-serving admonishments of the flock for the knowledge necessary for them to become citizens in

God's kingdom. Other pastors trample the grass the sheep feed on by going over and over a few favorite scriptural passages and pet concepts. These pastors take great satisfaction in selfishly pursuing their own interests, puffing themselves up and feeding themselves at the flock's expense. They not only lose out on the kingdom themselves, but they also close the door so that others cannot enter.

Good shepherds lead the sheep to fresh pasture and then get out of the way. They let go of their self-interests and let the sheep graze on what God wants to feed them. This is what brings joy to the Lord, and it is the shepherd's true delight.

Naming the Sheep

Part of my (Rosie's) enjoyment of my sheep is giving them names. I do not name the sheep going to slaughter, however, and I do not name the other lambs right away. I wait for their personalities to develop a little bit. Then the name I give them both tells me who the mother is and is a term of endearment.

However, it is not necessary to name the sheep, because they respond to the voice of their shepherd rather than to their own names. Several years ago, when we moved from our home in Illinois, we needed to have our sheep transported to their new home before we departed for ours in Washington. Our friend, John, came over with his truck to get them. The sheep were scattered about, so I called, "Sheep," and they all came running. We loaded them up, and John trucked them to his place about half a mile away. The next morning we got a phone call. It was John. "I don't know what's wrong," he said. "I unloaded the sheep into the pasture and they took off all over the place grazing up a storm. This morning I went out to get them all into one section of the pasture and they wouldn't come. I kept yelling, 'Sheep,' but they just ignored me!" The sheep did not know his voice.

Jesus, the Good Shepherd, names his sheep, and they know

his voice (John 10:2-4).[9] Jefferson says in *The Minister as Shepherd* that the undershepherds who know Jesus' voice and listen will hear him say:

> Feed my sheep. They are not yours. Not one of them shall ever pass from my possession, but I am going away ... and I leave them with you. Guard them, feed them, guide them, be good to them for my sake. Follow me. Remember my gentleness, my watchfulness, my considerateness, my patience, my compassion, my readiness to help, my swiftness to heal, my gladness to sacrifice. Be the kind of shepherd to my lambs and my sheep that I have been to you. Follow me![10]

For Reflection and Discussion

1. What aspect of life in your church do you value the most? Why is that?
2. Many different pastures can provide nourishment. How many can you identify in your church?
3. Glenn Wagner's "covenant community" offers many contrasts to the business model. Which positive contrast is best modeled in your church? Which one does not seem to be positive at this time?
4. Jesus did not say to count or fleece his sheep. What *are* the things that Scripture says are to be done with sheep?
5. The shepherd is also a sheep. Why is that so important to keep in mind?
6. Psalm 123:1-2 says, "I lift my eyes to you, O God, enthroned in heaven.... We look to the LORD our God ... just as servants keep their eyes on their master, as a slave girl watches her mistress for the slightest signal." Relate these verses to the thought that connectedness is needed between the one who shepherds and the Good Shepherd. What would you expect to see as evidence of connectedness?
7. What negative methods and results might you expect

from a pastor with a CEO mentality?

8. What positive methods and results would you expect from a church that has a "spring sheep" mentality?

9. Since sheep thrive on fresh foliage, "trampling the pasture" is inexcusable. Name some methods you have used or observed that help to keep things fresh.

10. Sheep naturally flock together. When one separates itself from the flock, what does that signal? Do you know who in your congregation is doing this? What are you going to do about it?

Getting Started

Choose two that you think could make a difference:

1. Compare the worship service and the Sunday school class attendance. Are you satisfied with the balance? What might be contributing to an imbalance: time, day of week, location, teacher/leader, subject(s)? What change(s) might be profitable?

2. Choose two or more people from the congregation and let them assess how well they are being fed in accordance with the seven questions on page 28. If different pasture management is needed, decide who is going to lead them there.

3. Does your church have an event mentality? a CEO mentality? a winter sheep mentality? Are you comfortable with this? If not, develop action plans to make the appropriate changes.

4. Is there evidence that the pastor is spiritually abusive and trampling the pasture the sheep feed on? Consult resources such as *Wounded Workers,* by Kirk E. Farnsworth (WinePress, 1998), for direction.

4

gathering

---

ideas for IMPROVING your church's ministry

11. An action plan to fulfill God's grand purpose: gather and go
12. Five dramatic differences between what "new" and "old" churches communicate to help you choose your style of "doing" church

---

We love to visit our children and grandchildren. With great distances involved, our trips are infrequent but regular. We anticipate, plan, and prepare, and we always try to take something with us to give to them—a box of freshly picked apples or our homemade apple cider, even a hand-sewn "baby" quilt for our youngest grandchild.

We could easily regard family gatherings as the greatest gift God could bestow upon us as a family and consider the family itself as God's greatest blessing to us as individuals. Yet the Lord offers us even more: gatherings of God's family. We cherish that God regularly draws us into his presence for his purpose.

Gathering is second on our list of ten biblically life-transforming activities that produce healthy churches. Every time people in the church come together, God has drawn them together for a divine purpose. This is important to keep in mind. Here the small church has the advantage in being a church family, wherein no one lacks a family and church members' family gatherings can move beyond the relational to the communal.

Church Family Gatherings

When we look at Scripture, we see that Jesus transformed the whole concept of family. Diana Garland sets the stage for us in her masterful book *Family Ministry:* "Americans usually think of the 'model' family as a husband and wife with their own biological children. Jesus' birth and teachings challenge this. Family, according to Jesus' own lineage ... now means adoption, not simply biological relationship."[1]

Garland provides for us the first core value of the transformed view of family. As Christians we are joint heirs with Christ, adopted into God's family regardless of our human alliances and biological relationships (Romans 8:17). Our faith in Jesus is proof of our kinship; we are members of God's family.

God's family, bound by faith rather than by flesh and blood, is the church universal and particular. The local church is the ultimate fulfillment of God's promise: "A father to the fatherless, a defender of widows, is God in his dwelling. God sets the lonely in families" (Psalm 68:5-6, NIV). Moreover, Jesus said, "I will build my church, and all the powers of hell will not conquer it" (Matthew 16:18). Therefore, no one in the church lacks a family, either now or ever. This is the second core value of the transformed view of family.

The third core value is that everyone has his or her own place in God's family, the church. *Everyone has a unique place.* The church to which we belong is not meant to be a family of clones, in which we relate to one another with undifferentiated sameness, without preference and without recognition of individual worth. God himself loves us particularly, not identically. Ray Anderson and Dennis Guernsey keenly observe in *On Being Family* that "if God loved everyone equally, then he would love no one particularly. This is indeed scandalous! ... The basis for love ... is not equality as an abstract and inclusive concept, but 'being chosen' as a particular and unique relation to the one who loves."[2]

Our uniqueness in the family of God has no higher point of reference than the words spoken especially to eunuchs: "I will give them an everlasting name that will not be cut off" (Isaiah 56:5, NIV). What could be a stronger guarantee of one's future? Certainly passing on the family name or being remembered by one's children would not even come close to an everlasting guarantee.

The Importance of Singleness

The same holds for everyone, of course, regardless of marital or parental status. Hope for the future is an especially sensitive issue for single adults who are situated outside the "model" American family. It doesn't help that being single certainly is not a privileged position in the church today, where singles are typically defined more by who they are *not* rather than by who they are. However, singleness is potentially the clearest witness in the church for the fact that one's future is not guaranteed by the biological family but by the church. This guarantee—whether one is married, unmarried, a single parent, or widowed—is the resurrection.

In *Families at the Crossroads,* Rodney Clapp speaks of singleness as uniquely important to the church because of the radical witness to the resurrection by those who put their total trust in God:

> The married Christian ultimately *should* trust that his or her survival is guaranteed in the resurrection; the single Christian ultimately *must* trust in the resurrection. The married, after all, can fall back on the passage of the family name to children, and on being remembered by children. But singles

mount the high wire of faith without the net of children and their memory. If singles live on, it will be because there is a resurrection. And if they are remembered, they will be remembered by the family called church. Christian singles are thus radical witnesses to the resurrection.[3]

The transformed view of family is more evident in a small church than in a large church. Large churches have many programs for various age groups and life situations (such as singleness) that pull people in different directions rather than weaving them together into a transformed faith family. "A congregation of a thousand people—or even two hundred—cannot really be family to one another except in the sense of extended family," says Garland.[4] Church family gatherings should not be family reunions of relative strangers.

What Are You Gathering to Do?

What should church family gatherings be like? That is, how do people in your church describe what they do in church? Following are some things we have seen and heard through the years that tell the story of many small and large churches alike:

1. Sitting in the pew tops the list of what people see themselves doing when they go to church.
2. Following along, which people in contemporary styles of worship do as they seem to follow mindlessly (the best they can) as the worship team presents a nonstop concert of praise until the time comes for the pastor to preach. So the service proceeds, moving to its own predetermined conclusion. One could easily conclude that if the congregation never showed up, it would not make any difference whatsoever.
3. The congregation sings what it is told to sing, when to sing, how to sing, when to stand, and when to sit.
4. Fellowship is a very common term, but often a very superficial experience of social interaction without spiritual intention.

5. Meetings in churches include attending Sunday school
    classes that have low expectations for student preparation
    and participation, committee meetings that often are
    unnecessary, and business meetings that rubber-stamp
    decisions already made.

Small churches need to capitalize on their inherent family
advantages. Yet one woman who faithfully attended a large
church for many years before making the change to The
Gathering Church had this to say: "I'm finally being fed. I
did everything the other church offered. I never missed. I sat
in the pew regularly for eighteen years. But as I think back, I
cannot think of one thing that I learned. All I got was warm
fuzzies, not the deeper worship and in-depth teaching that I
get here. I've learned more in one class here than in all those
eighteen years." In the past, she wanted nourishment. Instead
she got entertainment.

Too often, people see going to church as individually going
to a building to sit in a pew, to follow mindlessly along, to sing
on cue, to interact superficially, to sit through classes and
committee meetings, and to rubber-stamp decisions. Then
they go home. A church family gathering, however, should
not revolve around merely a facility to go to but rather around
a family to belong to. It is people assembling for meaningful
and purposeful connection and involvement. The orphan, the
homeless, and the outcast are all adopted as joint-heirs with
Jesus in the church family gathering. No one lacks a family;
everyone has a place.

Gathering and Going

Who? What? and *Why?* are questions before us. We have
already established who is gathering as a church. The church
gathers as family, where everyone who accepts Jesus is adopted as a joint heir with him.

Later chapters will focus on what people do in church. Here we focus on the question of *why*, or for what purpose, church family gatherings occur.

We do not merely gather under our own power or volition. The Lord brings us together. We do not just meet together. The Lord *gathers* us. So for those who wake up on Sunday morning and say, "I don't think I'll go to church today. I'm too tired," or "I don't need to go to church to be a good Christian or to worship, because I can worship at home," or "This is my only day off and I need to get caught up around the house and do things with the family"—whatever the excuse, they have not heard or heeded the Lord's voice.

Gathering together because God calls us to do so is a matter of obedience. When people obey God's call, they are gathered into his name, for the sake of his name. *God* is the reason for the gathering. We do not gather for our own sake, whatever our individual or corporate needs might be. We gather for the Lord's sake. Jesus said, "For wherever two or three are gathered (drawn together as My followers) in (into) My name, there I AM in the midst of them" (Matthew 18:20, Amplified). *In Jesus' name* is more than a sign that we are Christians or a stamp of approval. When we gather in Jesus' name, he is drawing us into his powerful presence. Indeed, there is power in the name.

Gathering for a Specific Purpose

In *Return to Worship,* Ron Owens gives us further biblical perspective on assembling or gathering God's people:

> From Scripture and church history, we see that the gathering—whether in cathedrals, huts, or forests—was a meeting of the saints to worship God. At the gathering they worshiped through music, the reading of Scripture, and prayer.... At the gathering they met around the Lord's table to remember His death; at the gathering they asked

their questions and had fellowship with one another. These meetings were expressly for believers.

Over the course of Israel's history, the people were often summoned by their leaders to hear a word from God. Sometimes these were messages of instruction or warning, and sometimes "the gathering" was for a time of corporate repentance, worship, or celebration. Whatever the purpose, the summons was to *God's people* to gather. The gathering was for a special people with a specific purpose.[5]

We can clearly see gatherings for specific purposes in the Book of Acts. According to Oliver McMahan in *Becoming a Shepherd,* the church in Acts was a "gathering" church, where God's people gathered:[6]

- For fellowship, worship, and blessing
- In response to persecution
- To minister to one another
- For missionary and evangelistic work
- To resolve issues
- For times of commissioning

God gathers his people, drawing them into his presence, for a specific purpose. When God is not central to the entire process, however, things go radically wrong. Some worship services, for example, are regularly devoted to evangelism of the lost. Gathering solely for that purpose is fine, of course, but it is not much of a worship service as such. When all you can remember afterward is the altar call, and when your thoughts have been directed mostly to your own unworthiness rather than to God's supreme worthiness, you have not truly worshiped.

Another example of gatherings that miss God's mark are worship services that primarily serve the purpose of hearing the pastor preach. We have sat through sermons *ad nauseam* that attempted, with styles varying from boasting to boring, to feed our souls with psychological insights for living. We have quickly changed the channel when we saw a television preacher cranking up his wildly enthusiastic assembly of true believers and beginning to feed their appetite for health and wealth with the prosperity gospel. We have also suffered through distribution of voter guides and series of sermons plugging political agendas weeks (even months) before an election.

We must face an inescapable conclusion. When worship services are sermon-centered and every other aspect of the service is geared toward the sermon, the inevitable result is an audience held hostage by projection of the pastor's personality rather than worshipers practicing the presence of God. This is not true worship.

Other examples abound. Suffice it to say that when God gathers us into his presence to worship *him* and we divert our focus to something else, God is displeased. Focusing in a gathering for worship on evangelizing the lost or the pastor's preaching or healing the wounded, whatever it is, is not what God intended. Rather, God's specific purpose for us is to praise, adore, and bless the Almighty God, to glorify his name. In short, we are to focus on worshiping the Lord!

A church gathers in many ways for many purposes: worship, prayer, fellowship, Bible study, youth and small group gatherings, committee and board meetings, and more. Each gathering should try to be true to its specific purpose. We have seen so many worship gatherings embracing the things of God without genuine passion for God himself. Typically, people at prayer gatherings talk a lot about prayer requests but do little actual praying. Bible study gatherings are more about socializing than about studying. Youth gatherings focus more on entertainment than on character development.

Gathering for God's Grand Purpose

Another problem is evident. When people gather primarily to meet their own needs and with their own agenda, apart from

God's specific purpose, they tend to become satisfied with themselves and with their results. They become complacent and comfortable, in-grown and self-absorbed. They have missed God's grand purpose.

God gave to every gathering of God's people one grand and universal purpose. Jesus said to the disciples, "Go then and make disciples of all the nations, baptizing them into the name of the Father and of the Son and of the Holy Spirit" (Matthew 28:19, Amplified). On that occasion, he had gathered them at a mountain in Galilee. Once they were drawn into Jesus' presence, they fell down and worshiped him. This was God's special purpose for their gathering. Then Jesus gave them another purpose, a grander purpose: Go. Gather for worship; then go and make disciples (Matthew 28:16-20). *Gather and go.*

This has been the biblical pattern ever since. When the church was born, the apostles remained in Jerusalem, as Jesus commanded them, gathered in an upper room to wait for the gift of the promised Holy Spirit. The Holy Spirit came upon them and filled them, and they went out into the city empowered to carry forth the good work the Lord had begun in them (Acts 1–2). God clearly had a special purpose and a grand purpose. Wait on the Lord and be filled with the Holy Spirit; then go and make disciples. Gather and go.

Throughout the New Testament, in the epistles particularly, gatherings of saints are instructed concerning their relationships with God, with one another, and with the world outside their Christian communities. In the contemporary church, when these things are learned and applied in individual lives, people are being discipled. This is the "making disciples" part of Jesus' command to go.

Chuck Colson warns the modern church in his book, *The Body,* that *"the church must be the church.* Away with consumer religion, the edifice complex, slick marketing plans, and syrupy sermons. Equip the people of God with spiritual weapons so they may serve the living God in the world."[7] Indeed, our vision of the church being the church is God drawing God's people into God's presence for the purpose of equipping and empowering them for ministry—and then sending them out as God's disciples and witnesses to the saving grace of Jesus Christ. God draws us in, equips us, and then sends us out. That is how God works. If you really want to see God at work, identify for each type of gathering in your church an action plan to gather and go.

Where Are You Gathering?

A few years ago, author Tim Stafford visited a wide spectrum of new churches to find out the latest trends in new church buildings and the beliefs of the people who built them. "All church buildings tell stories about the people who build them and about their understanding of how God meets his gathered people," Stafford wrote in an article for *Christianity Today*.[8]

First, he found that new churches put much more emphasis on how people arrive and depart, while older churches were built with very little concern for the welcoming transition between sidewalk and sanctuary. He also found much greater emphasis on improved communication through sound and video technology in the newer churches. He found that displaying the pastor on a big screen has replaced displaying Jesus on stained glass. He furthermore found some dramatic differences between what "new" and "old" churches communicate. (Keep these in mind as you choose your style of "doing" church.):

- Purpose, practicality, and pleasantness vs. sanctuary, sacredness, and solemnity
- Modesty (functional platform and informal worship space) vs. majesty (raised pulpit and formal pews)
- Community (participation of God's people) vs. hierarchy (dispensing of sacraments and truth by professional clergy)

- Connectedness (semicircular seating) vs. ceremony (long rectangular seating)
- Reaching outward (seeker friendly) vs. reaching upward (transcendence of God)

Second, Stafford found that the horizontal and the vertical are inextricably linked and that one is not necessarily better than the other. We must remember that we are a covenant community, reaching out to the surrounding community while standing on the firm foundation of the gospel and reaching up to the Lord, our hope of glory. We can easily forget this. "The very meaning of 'the people of God' has a fragile hold on Christians' consciousness," Stafford observes. He continues, "It is extremely important that we connect with one another, building our identity as disciples together. In a way that our grandparents did not, we need to go to church to express our identity as the people of God and to be persuaded anew that Jesus is Lord."[9]

Third, Stafford found that bigger churches do not necessarily have better worship services. Worshipers in smaller churches, when they are seated in semicircles, can move beyond the relational to the communal. They are able to hear one another speak, sing, and pray. They look one another in the eye as they worship and see God moving in people they know and love. Smaller churches may not be able to afford all-electric auditoriums, but they also don't have to endure the overwhelming intrusiveness of the sound amplification system.

Stafford points out that people come to church basically to hear the pastor and for the music. That is not good enough. Stafford accurately observes, "Music remains vital to worship, but mainly by way of electronic sound broadcast from the platform. The congregation participates, but ... their voices are neither needed nor heard. The music [merely] functions as an auxiliary to the pastor's message. The congregation [merely] expresses agreement by singing along."[10]

Stafford's analysis clearly concludes that new is not necessarily better than old, nor is big necessarily better than small. Nor does "small" equate with "old." Great, untapped potential exists in both the new and the old, as God meets his gathered people in the small church.

For Reflection and Discussion

1. Scripture refers to believers as *flock, army, body,* and *temple*. What aspects of the church as *family* connect with your thinking?
2. Some churches are full of people who are like ships passing in the night. How would you describe the interaction of the people in your church?
3. What do you believe is the importance of singleness to healthy churches?
4. Imagine telling someone who does not attend your church about the worship service. How would you describe what and whom your church focuses on when you meet?
5. Believers gathered in the early church purposefully and were empowered by the Holy Spirit (Acts 1–2). Which of the six types of gatherings of the church in Acts (p. 48) does your church do faithfully and well? Why is that?
6. No matter their size, many churches will continue to do exactly the same things as always, whether or not the Holy Spirit "shows up." What things during a worship service indicate to you that the service is not being guided by the Holy Spirit? What about other types of church gatherings?
7. Select two or three types of gatherings in your church and provide an example of God's special and grand purpose for each.
8. What part of Tim Stafford's research regarding trends in new church buildings came as a surprise to you? Why do you think that is a trend?

9. Sketch out some possible seating arrangements for worship in your church, with or without pews. What are the strengths and weaknesses of each?
10. Why do you gather with believers?

Getting Started

1. Survey the single adults in your congregation to determine their feelings about being part of God's family and having a unique place in the church. Ask them to identify any changes that might need to be made to make that happen.
2. Write a purpose statement for each type of gathering in your church. Be sure to include God's special and grand purpose for each.
3. Construct your preferred style of "doing" church from Tim Stafford's five choices between "new" and "old." How does it differ from your church's present style?
4. Develop a mini-survey that will ask as many members of the congregation as possible why they gather with other believers for worship, for prayer, and for Bible study. Relate their answers to God's purposes for those types of gatherings.

5

covenanting

---

ideas for IMPROVING your church's ministry

13. A sample church covenant
14. Guidelines for eliminating politics from church governance
15. Guidelines for making the sacrament of Communion,
    faithful tithing, and the regular gathering together of
    believers central to covenantal living

On display in St. Patrick's Cathedral in Dublin hangs an
ancient door with a rough-hewn, rectangular opening
hacked in the center. The story of this "door of reconciliation" and the related Irish expression of "chancing one's
arm" are remarkable and instructive. Almost five hundred
years ago, in 1492, two prominent Irish families, the
Ormonds and Kildares, were in the midst of a bitter feud.
Besieged by Gerald Fitzgerald (Earl of Kildare), Sir James
Butler (Earl of Ormond) and his followers took refuge in
the chapter house of St. Patrick's Cathedral, bolting themselves in. As the siege wore on, the Earl of Kildare concluded that the feuding was foolish.

Here were two families worshiping the same God in
the same church, living in the same country, trying to
kill each other. So he called out to Sir James and, as an
inscription in St. Patrick's says today, "undertook on
his honour that he should receive no villanie." Afraid of

"some further treachery," Ormond did not respond. So Kildare seized his spear, cut a hole in the door, and thrust his hand through. It was grasped by another hand inside the church. The door was opened and the two men embraced, thus ending the family feud.[1]

I (Kirk) am sitting here—on St. Patrick's Day—pondering this extraordinary story. It forms a poignant backdrop for a contemporary version that is also on my mind. Two Christian women from another church are feuding and are emotionally barricaded from one another. A third woman, from our church and a friend of both the other women, has been trying to bring them to a door of reconciliation but without much success. What is striking to me is that our church is a covenanting church, while the other church obviously is not. It is natural for the woman from our church, therefore, to think in terms of believers risking an arm to reconcile a relationship.

The determination in this story from St. Patrick's Cathedral, where a rough hole was hacked through a heavy door and a vulnerable hand thrust through, to be grasped by another hand from the inside, is a powerful illustration of covenanting. When nothing can stop two feuding families from reconciling—families that worship the same God and belong to the same church—we are witnessing covenanting.

Why has the power of covenantal living largely been lost in the church today? Has the church lost interest in creating an atmosphere of love and of faithfulness to promises with a common purpose? This is our definition of covenanting, the third of ten biblically life-transforming activities that produce healthy churches. The small church has the advantage in covenantal living. It focuses on disciple-making, mutual accountability, solemn commitment to the body of Christ, a strong sense of belonging to God's family, and taking politics out of church governance.

Living the Covenant

Ask people why they chose their present church. What tops the list? The pastor, music, fellowship, youth program, nursery, location, or, maybe even the easy parking? Any of those would be pretty discouraging when one considers Chuck Colson's remarks in *The Body:*

> Rarely do we hear believers say, "I decided to join this church because of its character as a holy community." Nor do most choose a church on the basis of its capacity to disciple and equip them for ministry. Yet that should be our very first consideration. If the church is the Body, the holy presence of Christ in the world, its most fundamental task is to build communities of holy character.[2]

Colson is saying essentially that most people do not expect much from their church and their church does not expect much from them. This statement is sadly true for many people and churches, more than we care to admit. According to Colson, a definite trend has emerged: Churches that have the lowest expectations and are the least demanding are in the greatest demand. The worst-case scenario is churches simply competing for people's leisure time.

Communities of Holy Character

Healthy churches are high-expectation communities of holy character. In this type of community, according to Colson, "we commit ourselves to intimate relationships with fellow believers and submit ourselves to accountability, duties, and responsibilities. In this community our Christian character is shaped; it is the context in which our spiritual gifts are developed and exercised. It is the family whose ties cannot be broken."[3] This solidly describes a community of covenanting believers.

Covenanting is a process of steadfast love and faithfulness to a set of promises with a common purpose—to a covenant—

for the mutual benefit of all who make the commitment. A covenant is a vow, a solemn commitment that we make with and before the Lord. A true covenant is *not* a covenant of convenience. It is not a casual commitment, a promise kept only when it is convenient to keep it.

Contractual Mentality

Those who make covenants are not independent contractors, committed primarily to themselves and their own rights and obligations. Important differences exist between a covenant and a contract. Contracts follow the business model. In contrast, covenants follow the biblical model. They create an atmosphere of giving rather than getting, of receiving what we need rather than receiving what we think we deserve. Covenanting creates an atmosphere wherein we do not dwell on what the church "owes" us or what church members owe one another. Covenants are *not* agreements that last only as long as each gets his or her needs met.

It is not hard to find people in most churches who have a contractual mentality. These persons are typically high-maintenance, low return people. Some do not contribute either through ministry time and energy or finances but still want the people in the church to respond to their every need. Some begrudge the church for not doing the things for them they think they deserve. Others leave the church when church members fail to do for them what they expect and then have trouble reconnecting elsewhere.

We see a clear difference between those who live by contract and those who live by covenant. Contractors make a casual commitment to the church body and protect their own interests with their own thoughts to guide them. Covenantors keep from their heart a solemn commitment to the church body with passion for God and for the welfare of God's people.

Covenantal Relationships

Covenantal relationships among individuals within the body include all of the following characteristics. They are:

- Based on commitment
- Bound together in love
- Built around promises with a common purpose
- Bathed in passion from the heart

Individual believers are neither forced into covenantal relationship with the church, nor with other believers within the church. In either case, covenantal relationships are freely offered and freely chosen. They form most naturally in communities of holy character, where intimate relationships thrive in the midst of church family ties that ultimately cannot be broken. Covenanting brothers and sisters in Christ risk an arm to reconcile a relationship. Covenantal love provides more opportunities to give than to receive. In short, as Bill Hybels said when speaking of developing today's leaders, covenantal relationships are God's provision to meet our deepest needs:

- To know and be known
- To love and be loved
- To serve and be served[4]

Renewing the Covenant

From day one of our official beginning, The Gathering Church has used a membership covenant. The form we presently use is reproduced below.[5]

Having placed our faith in the Lord Jesus Christ, we do now in the presence of God and this gathering solemnly and joyfully enter into this covenant with one another as one body of Christ.

We covenant by the aid of the Holy Spirit:

In Building the Church:

1. To unite with others in mutual labor for the Kingdom

2. To join in the advancement of The Gathering Church as a community of holy character

3. To sustain The Gathering's commitment to corporate prayer, study and worship

In Giving:

1. To give God His tithes and our offerings cheerfully and regularly, as God provides, to the support of The Gathering and its world-wide ministry

In Daily Living:

1. To endeavor to maintain regular Bible study and family devotions

2. To walk circumspectly in the world

3. To be just in all personal dealings and faithful in all personal engagements

In Caring for Others:

1. To care for one another in Christian love

2. To remember others in prayer and to aid them in sickness and distress

3. To be slow to take offense and always ready for reconciliation

In Witnessing:

1. To witness faithfully to the saving and keeping power of Jesus Christ

2. To endeavor to bring to a saving knowledge of Christ all who are within our personal sphere of influence

Although Thom Rainer reports in *High Expectations* that only a few churches actually require the signing of a church covenant, he notes that those that do are the healthiest churches.[6] At The Gathering, we give the opportunity to sign the covenant annually. This serves several purposes:

• Reviewing the covenant
• Renewing the covenant
• Maintaining membership
• Maintaining eligibility for leadership

- Opening the door for private discussion with those who have not been keeping the covenant or do not sign the covenant

Membership

Signing the covenant each year helps The Gathering communicate high expectations and offers the opportunity for covenantal life to all who attend, not just those who are official members. We try to have people covenant first and become members second. This means that a person may have signed the covenant but is not yet a member, but a person cannot become a member without signing the covenant.

Covenanting involves people. It is relational. Most significantly, covenanting makes us one with the heart of God and is a vital aspect of a healthy church, while membership, usually coming later, is part of the church's organizational structure. People *join* organizations; they *belong* with and to other people.

Membership is important in the covenantal life of the church. Most importantly, it provides the opportunity for governing or leadership positions, the privilege of voting, and accountability to corrective discipline.[7] Members are more than just consumers, and membership is more than mere concurrence with church doctrines and commitment to serving in church ministries. At The Gathering, membership is based on covenantal living and completion of core courses that establish unity of belief (orthodoxy) and develop a solid base for living the Christian life (orthopraxy). These core courses have no prerequisites or prescribed order; thus each person may take them in a timely, personally responsible manner. (We have more to say about core courses in Chapter 7.)

High expectations and membership go together in another highly predictable way. In *The Consumer Church*, Bruce and Marshall Shelley note that high numbers of members and lower expectations of those members to submit to biblical standards for following Christ are typical of big churches, while high expectations and lower membership numbers are typical of small churches.[8] Becoming a fully devoted follower of Christ takes time. It takes learning, worshiping, praying, and ministering together, all of which take place best within a covenant community of faith. Again, the advantage goes to small churches.

Selecting the Leadership

High expectations also fit nicely with Rick Warren's "Circles of Commitment" concept from his book, *The Purpose-Driven Church*.[9] Other authors have collapsed the five circles into four and assigned typical percentages to the circles that comprise the informal structure of any given church:[10]

1. Community—people who live in the surrounding community but do not attend church
2. Crowd (60 percent)—people who attend irregularly and have fallen through the cracks
3. Congregation (30 percent)—people who come to church regularly and give faithfully
4. Core (10 percent) —people who are committed covenant keepers, including the church leadership

In a church with high expectations, the Crowd percentage would be lower and the Congregation and Core percentages would be higher. That indeed is the case with The Gathering. Presently, our Crowd is only 20 percent, our Congregation is 50 percent, and our Core is 30 percent. Increasing the size of the Core should be the goal of every church. The Core is where the vibrancy and vitality of God's people, gathering together into his presence and covenanting in an atmosphere of love and faithfulness to his purpose, is felt strongly and seen in evidence.

God selects the leadership from the Core (other than the pastors) of The Gathering. Our leadership group is called the Governing Core Group, or Core Group for short. To be eligible, a person must be a member who has signed the covenant and successfully completed all the core courses.

The selection procedure for Core Group members is remarkable and has been a huge blessing in and of itself to the people of The Gathering. It is therefore worth describing in detail. First, nominations are placed in a nomination box by all who feel led by the Holy Spirit to do so. They are permitted to nominate as many people as they desire, including themselves. The pastor clears out the box each week of the one-month nominating period and notifies the individuals who have been nominated.

The pastor has this opportunity to communicate with those who are qualified regarding the expectations for serving on the Core Group. If they do not qualify, the pastor informs them that they are seen as having leadership potential and why they cannot be considered at this time. This type of nominating process motivates people and is an effective means of communicating high expectations. It also wonderfully relieves people from having to spend hours on nominating committees and, best of all, it removes politics from the nominating process.

The selection process itself takes place at our annual meeting. Before the meeting, bookmarks are put at the same place in as many hymnbooks as the number of qualified candidates. As many bookmarks as there are positions to be filled are marked in some special way. Then at the meeting, the hymnals are placed randomly on a table. We ask the candidates to stand as their names are called, so that we can pray the Lord's blessing on them as a group. We ask God to bless them for being willing to serve in this manner and for the Holy Spirit, knowing their hearts and schedules and what their circumstances will be during the coming year, to put together the right combination of people who can deal with whatever obstacles and opportunities may arise.

After all of the candidates have chosen a hymnal, they turn to a given page in their hymnal to discover whether the bookmark indicates that they have been selected. If so, they are asked to stand and are reintroduced as the new Core Group. Once again we pray for them. Politics are removed from the selection process because the Spirit has chosen by lot!

Some readers will object to this method, arguing that after the Holy Spirit came at Penetecost, no other Scripture tells of drawing by lot (Acts 1:21-26). We must therefore vote on important matters, because we now have the Holy Spirit. However, this is an argument from silence. Jesus says in reference to the Holy Spirit, "He lives with you now and later will be in you" (John 14:17). There has never been, nor will there ever be, a time when the Holy Spirit is absent. God does today what he has done in the past, so drawing by lot is a perfectly legitimate method for being led by the Holy Spirit in selecting church leadership.

We have described our Core Group selection procedure in some detail because of the power of covenanting that it portrays. Imagine a church where people do not lose elections. When we do not elect but let God select, no one loses. And imagine a church where people can nominate themselves for leadership positions if they feel God is leading them to do so, without feeling foolish or having to campaign to get elected. When people love one another and do not compete to seem more spiritual than one another, the covenant bond is strengthened and renewed.

Renewing and Breaking the Covenant

A covenant can be renewed or it can be broken. Biblical examples abound of renewing a covenant, including what Kingsley Fletcher points out in his book, *The Power of Covenant:*

> Moses renewed the covenant by *reading* it aloud before the people, by symbolically *sprinkling them with the blood* of the sacrifice, and by requiring the Israelites to *corporately*

and verbally pledge themselves to keep it in Exodus 24:7....
King David renewed his covenant with God after commit-
ting adultery and murder by *confessing* his sins, by *asking
for mercy and forgiveness,* by asking God to *"renew a
steadfast spirit"* within him, and by *offering the sacrifices of
a broken spirit:* a "broken and contrite heart" in Psalm 51
(Italics added).[11]

As Moses did, we too review our covenant corporately
and renew it by individually vowing to keep it. As King
David did, we too—after breaking the covenant—confess
our sins, ask for mercy and forgiveness, ask God to renew a
steadfast spirit within us, and offer the sacrifices of a broken
and contrite heart.

In the New Testament (Covenant), Jesus gave us the greatest
provision of all for renewing our covenant with him and with
one another, by instituting the sacrament of Communion on the
night he was betrayed (Luke 22:14-22). Fletcher aptly says:

> Every time we gather together in[to] Christ's name to
> share Communion, we are renewing and preserving the
> blood covenant of Jesus Christ that saves us, heals us,
> preserves us, unites us, keeps us and restores us to eter-
> nal fellowship with God our Father. This is the Lord's
> prescription for broken, weakened, fractured or strained
> covenant relationships.[12]

Just as a covenant can be renewed in many ways, so too, it
can be broken in many ways. Two ways of breaking a
covenant that are particularly harmful to the health of a small
church are withholding tithes and offerings and forsaking the
assembly of believers.

Withholding Tithes and Offerings

Have you ever thought of tithing as a covenant *privilege?* In
an article for *The Morning Star Journal,* Larry Ocasio calls
the tithe our privilege. He writes,

It is a requirement of the Lord that is not afforded to anyone but his own people. Nowhere in the Old Testament do we find God requiring any other nation to give tithes but the nation of Israel. Likewise, in the New Testament, as the church entered into covenant with Jehovah God, she also partakes of the commonwealth of Israel, thus inheriting this privilege of offering up the tithe.[13]

The apostle Paul helps us understand that before our faith in Christ, we were separated from God's people, Israel, and strangers to the covenant promises God made to them. But now, because we belong to Christ, we have been brought near to God and to one another. Jewish and Gentile believers alike. All members of God's family (Ephesians 2:11-19). We are in a commonwealth relationship of sharing in common our wealth in Christ Jesus, because he has shared his inheritance with us.

Before we were in Christ, we were on the outside and without hope. Now, in Christ, we are on the inside, recipients of his abundant life and covenant blessings. As we receive, we freely give as an expression of his life within us and our gratitude to him. The overflowing abundance of our commonwealth relationship with Christ is wonderfully portrayed in Malachi: "'Bring the whole tithe into the storehouse, that there may be food in my house. Test me in this,' says the LORD Almighty, 'and see if I will not throw open the floodgates of heaven and pour out so much blessing that you will not have room enough for it'" (Malachi 3:10, NIV).

Our commonwealth relationship with Christ is also powerfully portrayed when we share Communion. As we receive the bread and cup, we renew our covenant relationship with Christ. All that he is and has are at our disposal. In turn, Christ is free to use all that we are and have—all belonging to him—for God's glory. When we withhold our resources, we are breaking the covenant, and the floodgates close. Tithing is indeed a privilege.

Forsaking the Assembly of Believers

Second, when we do not gather with other believers, we break the covenant. Hebrews 10:25 says clearly, "Let us not neglect our meeting together, as some people do." This is far more serious than a casual Christian might think. The obsessive individualism of modern culture creates a mind-set that leads people to think, "I don't feel like going to church" or "It's a great day to get things done" and being with other believers goes out the window. They do not realize that they are subtly profaning the Lord's name by their attitude: "It's no big deal." Chuck Colson not-so-subtly gives us reason to reconsider the implications of our casual behavior:

To "profane" means to take the holy and make it common. To treat the sacred with irreverence. To take the Lord's name in vain—which comes from the Latin *vanus*, or "empty." How many times do believers do just that? Oh, perhaps we don't swear; swearing is too obvious. Instead, we profane the Name subtly.

We forsake our assemblies. Or when we do gather, we offer empty words of devotion. We sing hymns devoid of meaning. Our thoughts wander during corporate prayer. We expend loose God-talk on others…. We treat God as some distant, remote abstraction…. We do so at our peril. For the church is not His whim; it is His love for eternity. It is not a little business venture He founded two thousand years ago and now, in retirement, watches indulgently.[14]

Anytime we trivialize the holy, we are breaking the covenant. And yet, because of Jesus, we can be restored to covenantal living. Because of him, we are neither separated from God's people nor strangers to God's covenant promises. Individually and corporately, because of Jesus, God's restoration of his people is exactly the same today as it was in the days of King Solomon: "If my people who are called by my name will humble themselves and pray and seek my face and turn from their wicked ways, I will hear from heaven and will forgive their sins and heal their land" (2 Chronicles 7:14).

If we will:

- Humble ourselves
- Pray
- Seek God's face
- Turn from our wicked ways

God will:

- Hear us
- Forgive us
- Heal us

Praise God!

For Reflection and Discussion

1. God's people, whether Israel or the church, have always been in covenant. What are some things believers lose by not covenanting with one another?
2. When you or your family sought a church with which to affiliate, what factors helped to make your decision? How do those reasons compare with the ones Chuck Colson describes?
3. Explain the difference between *contract* and *covenant*.
4. Some would decry annually signing the covenant as "legalistic." What advantages can you see in doing it so often?
5. What are common results of people attending church with a contract mentality?
6. What should be the requirements for church membership?
7. Faithful giving is a major component of a covenanting church. How does it reflect God's character?
8. Profaning the Lord's name means making the holy common and empty. List some ways Christians subtly profane the Lord's name.

9. In the United States, churches have adopted democratic procedures from our national, not spiritual, heritage. If "winning" or "losing" could be removed from the process of choosing leaders in your church, how would people react?

10. Most people do not hack holes in doors to reconcile with other believers. What have you seen or experienced that the Holy Spirit has used in your congregation?

Getting Started

1. Using the sample covenant as a guide, write a covenant of membership for your church.

2. Review your requirements for membership. What are your expectations for submission of members to biblical standards for becoming fully devoted followers of Christ?

3. What positive and negative reactions would you expect your congregation to have if your leadership team were chosen by lot from qualified candidates? What would stop its implementation? Is that a significant hindrance? Why or why not?

6

ministering

---

ideas for IMPROVING your church's ministry

16. Three guidelines for defining the role of the pastor as "coach"
17. Ten questions that put the dependency model of ministry to the test
18. Three steps for redeveloping a church in decline
19. A recommendation to teach about and assess the spiritual gifts of every member of the congregation
20. Four guidelines for supporting people who are starting new ministries

---

A healthy small church is a covenant community, and community defines ministry. It is possible for a church community, if it is not healthy, to choke the life out of and stifle its ministries. Gilbert Bilezikian has written on "reclaiming the local church as community" in his book *Community 101:*

[Many Christians] express dissatisfaction with churches conducting their business as if it were a business. They compare the stilted and stultifying routines of their church life to the effervescent explosion of Holy-Spirit generated vitality that enabled the church of Pentecost to conquer the ancient world for Christ. They wonder with nostalgia where the power has gone. They realize that they have often become lost in a jungle-growth of unbiblical traditions that choke the life out of their churches and stifle their ministries.[1]

Ministry conversely defines community. Ministries can bring power and vitality to their church communities. Or, of course, they can drain the life right out of their church communities, perhaps by abusing people or misusing resources.

Do you wonder where the power has gone? Has your church become lost in a jungle-growth of unbiblical traditions that stifle your ministries? We believe the way to get on track is by equipping and mobilizing the saints for spiritual gifts–based ministry. We believe this is the best solution for revitalizing your church's efforts at ministering, which is the fourth of ten biblically life-transforming activities that produce healthy churches. The good news is that small churches have the advantage in creating an environment for each member to exercise spiritual gifts in ministry.

Ministers

The first question to ask is, "Who are the people doing the ministries?" It goes back to communities defining ministries. Typically, churches not only decide what the ministries will be, but also who will do them. The usual procedure is to choose the ministries and then to ask for volunteers to fill the positions. That's backward! The better—and biblical—option is to identify the ministers first.

Who are the ministers? No question weaves itself into the very fabric of the healthy church more deeply, and no question unravels the tapestry of the dysfunctional church more quickly. To respond, we must first examine the historical context. In a foreword to Greg Ogden's book, *The New Reformation*, Roberta Hestenes speaks of the ministry of all believers:

There are serious matters on the unfinished agenda of the [Protestant] Reformation that demand urgent attention in our own day. One of the most critical of these is ... "the ministry of all believers," whether lay or ordained, male or female. If, as the Reformers agreed, priesthood is no longer limited to the hierarchical few but is intended as God's gift and God's intention for all believers, what is the situation in regard to Christian ministry or service? Is it possible that it too belongs to all believers and that our present structures and patterns actually inhibit God's intention for the way the work of the church is to be done?[2]

Greg Ogden provides us with an extraordinarily penetrating and compelling analysis of the unfinished business of the Reformation. He argues convincingly that historically the church has been entrapped in institutionalism and clericalism. Together, these two terms define the church as two-storied and pastor-focused. In short, churches by and large have bought into the corporate business model of top-down leadership and trickle-down ministry, with near-total domination of professional ministry over lay ministry.

Small churches are particularly affected when the domination of the pastor creates people who, says Ogden, just pay their dues and "live out their lives vicariously through 'Mr. Wonderful' as if his faith and abilities were theirs."[3] Dominating pastors create passive people who want a pastor who can do everything. Then the only ministry they need to do is the minimum required to keep the doors open. Ogden assesses this pattern:

> Why is this? When a winsome, charismatic figure is our leader, we can live his energy. There is a certain transference of value. We feel good about ourselves because we are attracted to a representative and figurehead who embodies a corporate personality. This in turn places little personal responsibility on us, and therefore a minimum of personal initiative is required. The leader covers the bases for us. The role of the congregational member is

to be an enthusiastic supporter through verbal adulation and financial contributions.[4]

Clergy and Laity

The church should be known for its ministering sheep, not for one dominant sheep, or mighty shepherd—super sheep, perhaps, but not super priest or super pastor. Pastors are equippers and examples, and they are overseers, not overlords. They are not to "lord it over" but to serve (Luke 22:25-26). They are not to act like "little tin gods," which is J. B. Phillips's translation of "lord it over" in 1 Peter 5:3 *(Letters to Young Churches)*.

Yet in many contemporary churches, little tin gods do lord it over those they supposedly serve. These two groups—the haves and have-nots, the experts and the "are nots"—are called the clergy and the laity. We join countless others across the land in proposing that we get rid of the clergy and laity distinction as it is popularly used. Richard Lovelace's remarks on the subject in the late '70s, when he wrote *Dynamics of Spiritual Life,* are still true today:

> The model of congregational life in the minds of most clergy and laity is one in which the minister is the dominant pastoral superstar who specializes in the spiritual concerns of the Christian community, while the laity are spectators, critics, and recipients of pastoral care, free to go about their own business because the pastor is taking care of the business of the kingdom.[5]

The institutionalized church nurtures the clericalism that perpetuates the distinction where clergy become superstars and lay people languish in the pews as spectators. *All* of God's people are called to ministry. Biblically, no subcategory exists called "lay ministry." The biblical model is for everyone to partner together in ministry. All are ministers, with some functioning as servants to equip the others, as coaches do. Teams of ministers and coaches are a better model.

Coaches

Elton Trueblood suggested several years ago that the best modern equivalent for the word "shepherd" is "coach." He writes, "The glory of the coach is that of being the discoverer, the developer, and the trainer of the powers of other men. But this is exactly what we mean when we use the biblical terminology about the equipping ministry."[6] Twenty years later, Gilbert Bilezikian's normative model of ministry also envisions the pastor as a coach, "who discovers the potential talents of team members and enables them to take the field while cheering for them from the sidelines."[7]

What do the coaches do to equip the ministers? Ogden has discovered three ways that *equip* can be categorized biblically: *mend*, *establish*, and *prepare*.[8] *Mend* entails praying for the restoration of physical health, damaged emotions, and broken relationships. Expose and correct false teaching, confront the sinfulness in people's lives, and set them on the right course. Build up people's faith in their times of crisis. *Establish* means laying firm foundations in Christ by creating a dynamic learning environment for teaching God's Word and for regular personal Bible study. Model aspects of seeking first the kingdom of God. And *prepare* involves training people in the areas of their giftedness for the exercise of ministry in the church body, surrounding community, and world. Give them specialized training in the skills they will need to become self-motivated caretakers of their gifts.

Models of Ministry
Dependency Model

According to Ogden, the institutional entrapment of the church has created a dependency model of ministry: "What is this model? *Pastors do the ministry, while the people are the grateful (or not so grateful) recipients of their professional care*. Pastors ... are the all-knowing parent figures who provide the protection and nurture for their dependent children. But in this family, the children never grow up."[9]

Pastors must ask themselves, "Am I locked into a role that fosters dependency?" Following are some of the characteristics of such a role identified by Ogden:[10]

1. Omnicompetence – "I must be good at everything."
2. Distrust – "I am the paid professional."
3. Ego-enhancement – "Someone needs me."
4. Motivation by guilt – "What if people think I am lazy?"
5. Busyness – "I must be doing worthwhile things all the time."

Meanwhile, the people in the church should be asking themselves, "Are we locked into a role that fosters codependency?" Following are some of the characteristics of this role identified by Ogden:[11]

1. The ubiquitous pastor – "We're fortunate. Our pastor can do everything."
2. The resident expert – "The pastor does hospital visitation best, so he should do it."
3. The inspirational bandage – "Give me something inspirational to get me through the week."
4. The church as possession – "I go to Pastor Smith's church."
5. The professional minister – "After all, that is what we pay him for."

Remedial Model

When churches face a life-threatening crisis from ministry that has become corrupted by heresy or contention, Bilezikian recommends the remedial model. This is an emergency rescue operation where the cure is commensurate with the crisis. Under this model an outside "referee," using the guidelines in the pastoral letters of the New Testament (Paul's two letters to Timothy and his letter to Titus), appoints overseers or elders to replace the current leadership. The overseers invoke authoritarian methods to direct the affairs of the church to restore order. The purpose of this contingent, remedial model is to control unruly churches, save self-destructing churches, and help make sick churches healthy again. Then, Bilezikian warns, the church must move as quickly as possible into the normative model described in the following pages.

Another approach to the remedial model is the redevelopment approach. This is for churches that are not in crisis as such but that have lost their vision. We have found it helpful for churches in this condition to think in terms of the entire lifecycle of the church. Ken Priddy, in his seminar on church redevelopment, describes the life stages of a church as follows: birth to incline (grow) to recline (plateau) to decline. (The incline to recline and finally decline stages can also be described as going from stable to stagnant, to sick.)[12]

Helping the Declining Church

A church in *decline* is losing or has lost its vision and is on the way or has already become driven by structural demands rather than by a vision that pulls it along. The mentality of the leadership is to preserve the institution, and the primary corporate goal is survival. The corporate focus has shifted. Rather than meeting needs in the surrounding community, as in the past, the church now expects the community to meet the church's needs. Ministry has essentially been replaced by marketing. The church is in the business of raising money to preserve its infrastructure and facilities, and concern for reaching the lost is replaced by fear of losing the reached.

To recover from decline, according to Priddy, the church needs to pull apart unhelpful structures (destructure) as it works its way back toward revisioning its values and mission, and as it restructures based on the new vision. He recommends three steps:

1. Destructure by having a third party—district superintendent or paid consultant—help the church membership identify visionaries in their midst and negotiate authorizing them to conduct a revisioning process.
2. Revision how God wants to work and what he wants to accomplish through the church in the future.
3. Restructure based on the renewed vision and according to a new model for ministry and leadership.

We recommend the normative model. Given a worst-case scenario, if the church is in an advanced decline, then the preferred choice is the remedial model.

Helping the Reclining Church

When a church is in *recline*, its vision has faded, and it is driven more by program than by vision. It is stagnant. According to Priddy, what was formerly strategic is now programmatic. The same programs go on and on with the same people doing the same jobs. Nothing is new. Quality is the first thing to go. As it spirals down, people leave, so programs are cut and more people leave. At best, the number of new people coming in equals the number of people leaving.

A church in this condition needs to get beyond having its identity defined by programs. It can do so by revisioning and restructuring in accordance with a healthy model of ministry. This means getting everyone involved in ministry, as the Holy Spirit gifts and leads. The Holy Spirit distributes spiritual gifts for ministry, and every believer has at least one (1 Corinthians 12:11).

The Holy Spirit also directs believers to initiate their participation in ministry consistent with their giftedness: "Those who follow after the Holy Spirit find themselves doing those things that please God" (Romans 8:5, TLB). Clearly, this is what we might call bubble-up ministry, rather than trickle-down as in the dependency model.

Normative Model

The normative model of ministry calls for structures of ministry based on the spiritual giftedness of all the members. By contrast, the remedial model is not spiritual gifts–based and imposes stringent limitations on who may do ministry. The most comprehensive study ever conducted on church health concluded that gift-oriented ministry is the key indicator of church health (see Chapter 2). This is empirically solid ground. It is solidly biblical as well. In *The Purpose-Driven Church,* Rick Warren lists characteristics of every Christian as drawn from Scripture:

- Created for ministry (Ephesians 2:10)
- Saved for ministry (2 Timothy 1:9)
- Called to ministry (1 Peter 2:9-10)
- Gifted for ministry (1 Peter 4:10)
- Authorized for ministry (Matthew 28:18-20)
- Commanded to minister (Matthew 20:26-28)
- Prepared for ministry (Ephesians 4:11-12)
- Needed for ministry (1 Corinthians 12:27)
- Accountable for ministry and will be rewarded according to his or her ministry (Colossians 3:23-24)[13]

A consistent pattern may be traced throughout the New Testament describing the church as a community of love and oneness. According to Bilezikian, "A normal expression of this oneness is unrestricted involvement of all believers in the ministry of the community. Since this ministry is carried out with each individual contributing his or her spiritual gift, the expectation is for all to use their gifts to the fullest."[14]

Flock Mentality

The idea that everybody in the flock has a contribution to make reminds us of four-legged sheep, and the phenomenon known as "the flock mentality." Research on flocks of wild sheep shows that one sheep will lead the flock to water from its memory of the water's location. Another remembers where the good pasture is and will lead the flock there. And so it goes. It is easy to think of a bunch of sheep as being pretty dumb, being led around all the time by one dominant sheep. Each flock will have a dominant sheep, but that leadership will be relinquished from time to time for the good of the flock.

How can a church develop a flock mentality? Aubrey Malphurs, in *Planting Growing Churches for the 21st Century,* has outlined a helpful three-phase process.[15] The education phase comes first. Spiritual gifts are taught to every member of the congregation. Most people who attend The Gathering Church neither knew their spiritual gift initially, nor did they have any idea who the Holy Spirit is and what he does. Consequently, we do not teach about spiritual gifts without first teaching about the Giver of the gifts.

One of our core membership courses deals with the person and work of the Holy Spirit and spiritual gifts. The first part of the course covers who the Holy Spirit is and what he does. The second part exposes the class to the variety of gifts the Holy Spirit gives the church body. People gain from this a greater appreciation for one another. Also included is an assessment process for identifying each individual's spiritual-gift-mix, passion, and personality type. At this point, Malphurs says, "Of the few churches that attempt some kind of program of assessment, most prematurely conclude with the first phase. This serves only to excite people and then kill their initial enthusiasm."[16]

The second phase is consultation. Again, we will use ourselves as our example. In order to receive credit for the Holy Spirit and spiritual gifts course, each person is expected to meet with a designated person—"consultant"—from within The Gathering. The purpose is to clarify their assessment results from the course and then to begin the process of finding direction for ministry. Different kinds of relevant options, both inside and outside the church, are discussed, and all of the pertinent information is passed on to the pastor for the final phase of the process.

The third phase is mobilization. Now that people know how God has wired them, they can see where he wants to plug them in. Connecting them with presently existing ministries either inside or outside the church is fairly straightforward. However, we have sometimes needed to encourage and support people in starting a new ministry outside the church, a very exciting and fulfilling process. Some guidelines are important to keep in mind:

1. This is not for "lone rangers" or those who wish to go it alone. A startup is much more effective if at least two people with a similar passion team up together.

2. "The most critical factor in a new ministry isn't the *idea*, but the *leadership*.... It is important never to push people into a ministry. If you do, you'll be stuck with a motivation problem for the life of the ministry. Most small churches get in a hurry and try to do too much," says Warren.[17]

3. Ownership or responsibility for new ministries should be assumed not by the church, but by those called to the ministries.

4. The concern of church leadership must be in preserving the freedom of believers to choose to serve the Lord. Coupled with that is offering encouragement and support, and perhaps insights and suggestions that might be helpful.

The heart of a healthy church is a covenant community with the coach equipping the ministers for building one another up in love and reaching out to the community and the world for Christ. Rather than monopolizing the ministry of the church, the coach multiplies ministers throughout the church. The ministers discover, nurture, and use their gifts in obedience to Christ and to the glory of God. That is the biblical model for ministry.

For Reflection and Discussion

1. Research and anecdotal evidence seem to indicate that fewer than 10 percent of the churches in the United States minister from a base of spiritual gifts. Why might it be that so few churches have found this to be a workable model?

2. What would you expect to see in a church that was practicing the motto, "Every one a minister"?

3. The statement is made at the beginning of the chapter that "community defines ministry." Reiterate what is said about that and then give reasons why you agree or disagree.

4. What did you learn about the clergy and laity distinction? What did you like or dislike?

5. Using the model of a coach for a team sport, how would you expect a pastor to interact with the "team" God has given him or her?

6. Which item(s) on the lists of characteristics of roles that foster dependency and codependency in the Dependency Model can you identify with?

7. Gilbert Bilezikian warns that the Remedial Model is useful for addressing a church's crisis situation, rather than for creating the norm for every church. What did you find disquieting or encouraging in that statement?

8. Is your church at the recline or the decline stage? If so, how might the redevelopment approach help your situation? If not, how might you avoid it in the future?

9. In the biblical foundation list for spiritual gifts–based, every-member ministry found on page 78, is there one or more you try to deny? Did one or more of the characteristics resonate with your spirit?

10. The authors give the example from their church of first teaching about the Holy Spirit—the Giver of gifts—before teaching about the gifts themselves. What strengths or weaknesses do you see in that approach?

Getting Started

1. Does your pastor have a job description? How would it read if it were written in terms of being a coach? Spell out what he or she must do to equip the ministers.

2. If your church is in recline (stagnant) or decline (sick), begin the redevelopment process by identifying visionaries in your congregation to develop a vision for ministry. Where is God already at work? What programs should be discontinued? Whose gifts can be uncovered so that more people can be involved in ministry? What would it look like for everyone to be involved in ministry?

3. To better understand the diversity of gifts, we recommend you have your leadership team read and apply Peter Wagner's book on how to discover your gifts and use them to bless others and build the kingdom (C. Peter Wagner, *Your Spiritual Gifts Can Help Your Church Grow*, Regal Books, 1994).

4. Be alert for hidden ministries in your church that could seem insignificant to the casual observer. How might these people be encouraged and supported?

7

studying

---

ideas for IMPROVING your church's ministry

21. Five essential guidelines for every student to form a Christian worldview
22. Six steps for internalizing what is taught
23. Four unique criteria for evaluating student learning
24. Guidelines for developing a curriculum for Christlikeness
25. Sixteen critical criteria to assess successful disciple-making

---

A. W. Tozer was a master at asking convicting questions. Here's one that is as true today as when he uttered it long ago: "Why should the Church of Jesus Christ be a spiritual school where hardly anyone ever graduates from the first grade?"[1]

Why, we must ask, should the majority of the people in our churches today remain in the darkness of biblical illiteracy? Why should they remain in the death grip of consumer Christianity, using God's grace for forgiveness and the good graces of their church in meeting their personal needs, but failing to learn constantly how to live their lives as disciples of Jesus?

As a whole, churches in the United States do not routinely teach people how to live their lives as disciples, or students, of Jesus. We lead them to profess allegiance to Jesus and leave them there. We devote ourselves to attracting them to the surface benefits of consumer Christianity. No wonder hardly anyone ever graduates from the first grade!

Living as students of Jesus and co-laborers with him in kingdom living is the great vision of the Great Commission, a vision that encompasses both evangelism and education. Jesus' charge to his disciples to go and make disciples is beautifully described in *The Message:* "Go out and train everyone you meet, far and near, in this way of life, marking them by baptism in the threefold name: you do this, day after day after day, right up to the end of the age" (Matthew 28:19-20).

The Great Commission describes the life and work of the church in educational terms. Every believer is to be a lifetime learner. Jesus has commanded *every* church to comprehensively and effectively teach *all* that he has commanded. This must go beyond acquisition to internalization, beyond knowing to believing. Jesus' disciples must not merely do what he would do, but live as he lived.

Education in the church is generally viewed as learning facts and applying them. However, Christian education will be much more than that if it consists of instruction in the practice of all that Jesus commanded. Nothing less is needed than a philosophy of education to guide our efforts. In the hustle and bustle of teaching Sunday school, we need to understand that teaching is not merely collecting and conveying information. Good teaching produces students who not only acquire knowledge and learn how to apply it, but who also act on what they have learned. They make decisions, accepting or rejecting what *is* in the light of what *ought to be.* We are teaching people who are learning to live as Jesus lived—not just stories and topics, issues and theology.

What does your church teach? How does it teach? Why? Are you building Christian education around making responsible decisions and making disciples? Consider focusing on these two goals at the youth and adult levels of study in your Sunday school program.

Studying is the fifth of the ten biblically life-transforming activities that produce healthy churches. Small churches have the advantage in adopting a philosophy of Christian education for people to become apprentices to Jesus in kingdom living within a family context rather than creating separate generational cultures.

Making Responsible Decisions

The first objective in the learning process is to teach the facts—facts pertaining to, for example, who God is, what Jesus has done for us, how the Holy Spirit works through us, and how Jesus builds his church and transforms his people. Second, the learners need to have the ability to acquire and apply knowledge, including the ability to read, listen, think clearly, and take action. Third, learners need to develop the inclination to apply what they learn.

If responsible action is a major goal in equipping disciples, then they will definitely need more than knowledge of the truth and the ability to apply it. They will also need to develop the tendency to apply it. In *Educating for Responsible Action,* Nicholas Wolterstorff calls this "tendency learning." By that he means developing an inner sense of habitual response, an intuitive sense for doing the right thing *before* giving it much thought.[2] Good teaching involves more than teaching biblical facts and how to apply them.

Christian Worldview Thinking

The most fruitful way to create a biblical context for tendency learning—to prepare the soil—is through forming a Christian worldview. According to Arthur Holmes in *The Making of a Christian Mind,* in order for a Christian worldview to be truly biblical, it must operate within the ongoing relationship between God and creation. "Within this relationship, God's providence is at work; so too are human sin and God's grace, Christ's Incarnation and his promised kingdom of justice and peace. The God-creation relationship then must be the overall biblical framework for Christian thinking and doing."[3]

Holmes specifies the following being-human-in-God's-creation components of a Christian worldview.[4] We list them as one example among many of the potency of a Christian worldview in the world we live in—in this case addressing the dominant popular emphasis on individualism:

1. We are relational, not isolated beings. We are not self-made, but live and work and have our being in our Creator. All issues of our life flow out of our relationship with God.

2. We cannot live alone as isolated beings. We are created to live in constant relation to nature and society. We are responsible to "handle with care" all aspects of God's creation.

3. We are created in relation to one another. We are *inter*dependent, not *in*dependent. We are responsible to scrutinize all social institutions—from marriage to government to the church—in light of pursuing God's purposes with justice, love, and peace.

4. We are to act responsibly in accordance with right values. We must continuously make value judgments throughout life. Therefore, Christian education must help us develop our capacity to think through life's issues and judge rightly, taking responsible action.

5. We must recognize the presence of sin and grace. We pervasively influence everything that we think and do when we sin—it is not merely an isolated, independent mistake. When we turn our backs on the God-creation relationship, we elevate the creature to the place of God and deny our own creatureliness. That strikes at the heart of being human. We must turn back to God's saving grace for healing and hope for the future.

The question is, How do we equip people to be predisposed or inclined, rather than just able, to act responsibly in accordance with their Christian worldview? Many pastors use preaching as the church's primary vehicle for teaching. They seem to believe that sermons are the best way to communicate how to develop a Christian worldview and how to apply it to the big issues of the day, as well as to inspire people to take responsible action. Wolterstorff, however, cites a series of studies that found that preaching falls far short of such lofty goals; it leads only to preaching, not to action. Preaching about living as Jesus lived therefore leads listeners only to preach about living as Jesus lived. With rare exceptions, preaching does not lead directly to responsible action. (More will be said in Chapter 8 about the limitations of preaching sermons.)

The problem with assuming that people will or will not do what we tell them is reminiscent of studies years ago of the effects of watching television on children. These studies found that children often do not learn what we think they were taught. In a study reported in *Psychology Today* all the way back in December 1969, children in one group watched a movie containing violence, while another group watched one without violence. Then the two groups were put into two separate playrooms for observation. Those who had viewed the violent movie were predictably much more aggressive and violent in their play activities. Even more than that, however, they learned not only how to be violent but to justify morally their behavior afterward.

Moral justification resulted from the children copying everything in the movie equally. They saw the good guy riding off into the sunset after bashing the bad guys, followed by a moral tag—words to the effect that crime does not pay. The goal, of course, was to neutralize the emotional effects of the violence and to discourage violent behavior. Instead of learning that the particular end justified the means, the children learned how to be violent *and* to rationalize it away. They learned to justify their violence![5]

No church wants to teach hypocrisy: "Do what I say, not what I do." People practice only what their teachers practice but tend only to repeat what they say. If we want to equip people for responsible action, the teachers must be acting responsibly in their lives—matching their actions to their words. Modeling is central to a healthy church's philosophy of Christian education.

Internalizing

What is *taught* (through word and deed) must also be *caught*. We cannot assume that if we teach and model responsible action, students will copy what we say and do. The chief concern for lifelong students of Jesus is internalizing all that he commanded. In other words, how can people be taught to act responsibly in accordance with Christian values without relying solely on external rewards and punishments? How can internal consequences, such as guilt, shame, satisfaction and pride, be included as motivators as well?

First, teach people a biblical framework—a worldview—for Christian thinking and doing, to know how to live as Jesus lived. Model the truth in your own life. But be sure to give people reasons—right values—with internal as well as external consequences for their actions. Wolterstorff documents the importance of reasons and adds that once a biblical worldview and biblical values have begun to be internalized, students will need opportunities to apply general biblical principles to specific, often perplexing cases where they have not yet developed a way of responding.

For example, should you forgive someone who is abusing you? Should you do something that is legal, even though it may not be ethical? How should you vote in a two-party political system where both parties advocate *some* Christian ideals and neither party is consistently Christian in its actions? Internalizing a Christian worldview means bringing general biblical principles to bear on specific predicaments such as these. Teachers must present in detail and practice with their students applying biblical principles to a variety of situations that they might face.

In *Educating for Responsible Action,* Wolterstorff recommends six steps in teaching people to apply biblical principles:[6]

1. Describe the facts. Facts are usually what are in dispute. They must be presented as accurately as possible and as elaborately as necessary.
2. Discover options. Choices are always available.
3. Eliminate options. Some options are obviously ruled out immediately when brought under the light of Scripture.
4. Predict consequences. Each of the remaining options must be seen in terms of their positive and negative effects. This might include asking students to take the role of others involved in the situation and consider how those people would feel.
5. Decide which biblical principles seem to apply. In World War II the Dutch who considered hiding Jews had to face several difficult questions that readily lent themselves to biblical analysis. Was it a case of misleading someone? Was it also a case of saving someone's life? In addition, was it a case of disobeying authority?
6. Prioritize applicable biblical principles (if necessary). The Dutch individually and repeatedly had to decide whether their responsibility to protect human life overrode their responsibility to tell the truth and to obey authority. They had to decide which biblical principle was most important.

These are the procedures for teaching tendency learning, that is, for educating people to be predisposed or inclined to act responsibly in accordance with biblical principles. How do we know that students are learning? Wolterstorff additionally lists four unique evaluation criteria:[7]

1. They resist pressure to deviate from their Christian world-view of life and choices.
2. They feel guilt upon deviating.
3. They avoid appealing to external sanctions when giving reasons for acting responsibly.
4. They confess and accept responsibility for deviating from applying biblical principles.

Just as importantly, how do we know that teachers are fulfilling their mission? Ecclesiastes 12:10-11 states, "The Teacher taught the plain truth, and he did so in an interesting way. A wise teacher's words spur students to action and emphasize important truths." We need to know that our teachers and students alike get it right.

Making Disciples

Dallas Willard proposes a "curriculum for Christlikeness" in his book *The Divine Conspiracy.* He believes we must not only teach information about what Jesus believed and practiced, but we must also train people in the formation of those things into their own lives.[8]

The primary objectives for Willard's curriculum are twofold:
1. "… to bring apprentices to the point where they dearly love and constantly delight … in Jesus and are quite certain that there is … no limit to the goodness of his intentions or to his power to carry them out."[9]
2. "… to free the apprentices … of 'enslavement' … to their old habitual patterns of thought, feeling and action."[10]

The First Objective

The first objective helps students know the Lord more clearly so they can love him more dearly, by abiding in the living words of Scripture and living in accordance with them. Jesus said to all who believe in him, "If you abide in My Word—

hold fast to My teachings *and* live in accordance with them—
you are truly my disciples" (John 8:31, Amplified).

We are intentional at The Gathering Church to create an
invigorating learning environment for abiding in God's Word.
Adult elective classes held over the course of three months last
one and a half hours and are interactive (as opposed to a lecture
format). They are at the center of Sunday morning activities—
along with prayer and worship. Five of the courses comprise our
"core course" requirements for church membership. They are:

- Growing Strong in God's Family
- Knowing What You Believe
- Experiencing God
- Discovering Your Spiritual Gift(s)
- Becoming a Contagious Christian

Other courses include a range of topics and books of the
Bible, for example, "Mastering Your Money" and "Satisfying
Work from Nine to Five," "Peacemaking" and "Intercessory
Prayer," "Sermon on the Mount" and "Jesus Among Other
Gods," as well as Ruth, Ezra/Nehemiah, Job, John, Romans,
and Ephesians. We continuously add new courses.

We believe in "intensive grazing." Each pasture our four-
legged sheep roam gets grazed completely. This helps keep the
grass healthy and controls the weeds. The same holds true
with our church courses. The subject matter is pursued in
depth. Rather than skimming off the tastiest tidbits and moving on, students have the opportunity to understand deeply
and apply what they learn. This keeps the course alive and
life-giving and helps students deal with weeds in their lives.

Another aspect of intensive grazing is keeping the old and the
young sheep together. This allows the old to teach the young
how to find nourishment. That is one good reason for keeping
older and younger people together in the same courses.

We do not ordinarily separate our courses by age except in
the children's department. We have everyone age thirteen and

older sign up for adult electives. All of our courses are interactive, giving all of our students the opportunity to learn from one another regardless of age. Young adults have the opportunity to observe older adults acting responsibly in accordance with Christian values. Younger people are encouraged when they can see how their questions are surprisingly similar to those of older people. They realize that they know more than they thought they did. They also gain respect from older people, and that is helpful for a teenager's parent(s) to see when they are in the same course. Each of these examples gives those who are older the additional opportunity to show their appreciation for those who are younger, and vice versa. The small church is just the right place for all this to happen.

We want teens to be equipped to be fully functioning members of the church, not just junior citizens sequestered in a parallel universe—a separate youth culture—who become adults not knowing what adult church is. The contemporary church, however, is constantly in a quandary over how to uniquely minister to "the new generation." Dennis Sawyer, senior pastor of Church by the Side of the Road, in Seattle, astutely observes in a *Christianity Today* article, "If everything for teens has to be specialized ... how do you keep their faith alive when they graduate from high school or college, and all the folderol stops? You've conditioned them for beach trips and lock-ins, and suddenly they're disappointed. We believe it's better not to set [up] teens in the first place."[11]

Andy Crouch, also in a *Christianity Today* article, believes that we would be better off taking seriously the biblical usage of the word "generation."[12] The Old Testament usually refers to the continuity between parents and children in passing on the faith. The New Testament usually refers to everyone who is alive at a given moment. Crouch says, "Both senses are vital to the church at this moment in history, whereas breathless hype about 'the new generation' is mostly useful to those whose jobs depend on convincing young people they have nothing in common with their parents."[13]

The church is not being the church when it segregates people according to age in order to "do" ministry. Good business is not necessarily good ministry. The church is just what Peter says: a special people, "a chosen generation, a royal priesthood, an holy nation" (1 Peter 2:9, KJV).

The Second Objective

The second primary objective of a curriculum for Christlikeness concerns the body more than the mind. Willard rightly points out that the mind must be transformed and the body must be transformed, and that is not accomplished by talking about it.

When Willard refers to transforming the body, he is talking about everyday, garden-variety habits. Many of these are knee-jerk reactions to impatience, self-centeredness, fear, anger, bodily desires, and the like. In *The Divine Conspiracy*, Willard writes:

> Typically, we have acted wrongly before reflecting. And it is this that gives bad habits their power.... It is rare that what we do wrong is the result of careful deliberation. Instead, our routine behavior manages to keep the deliberative will and the conscious mind off balance and on the defensive. That leaves us constantly in the position of having to deal with what we have already done. And the general "pattern of wrongdoing" that takes over in that case is to defend what we have already done by doing further wrong: by denying, misleading, and rationalizing—or even killing someone, as King David did.[14]

Bad bodily habits, as commonplace as they are, create just the right circumstances for Satan's handiwork. Christians should not be surprised that these supposedly "little things"— "little follies" that outweigh wisdom and honor, and "little foxes" that ruin the vineyards (Ecclesiastes 10:1; Song of

Solomon 2:15)—can provide such big openings through which Satan gains footholds in people's lives.

How can we change these habitual patterns? How can we replace wrong habits with automatic responses that reflect kingdom values? Christian education at its best will create in students tendencies to act responsibly, and it will also help them develop habits that support their right tendencies in "moments of truth." Good intentions point the way, but they must be supported by good habits.

Spiritual Disciplines

Willard recommends adding spiritual disciplines to our curriculum for Christlikeness. There are many disciplines and we will not attempt to list them all.[15] However, Willard sorts them into two useful categories:

1. **Abstinence:** Disciplines such as solitude, fasting, frugality, and sacrifice are included in this list. These disciplines are designed to disrupt and weaken the life involvements that feed our patterns of wrongdoing.

2. **Engagement:** Disciplines including study, worship, service, prayer, and fellowship. These disciplines are designed to help us, in Willard's words, "do from the heart the things that Jesus knew to be best."[16]

The two categories correspond closely with the contents of this book. What we call life-transforming activities of both mind and body for healthy people in healthy churches are in essence spiritual disciplines. Although both spiritual disciplines and life-transforming activities are absolutely essential to break bad habits and train for kingdom living, as Willard points out, such endeavors are not in and of themselves deeds of righteousness. Neither do those who practice the most spiritual disciplines or life-transforming activities get more points for being righteous. The righteous are known by their fruit.

Assessment of Successful Disciple-making

The fruit of the two primary objectives of a curriculum for Christlikeness can be seen in the following:

- Solitude that creates space in our thought life for the Holy Spirit to drive out the noisy interruptions of our inner voices and to keep out the subtle seductions of the outer voices of darkness
- Study that creates biblical boundaries within the inner space, giving us opportunities to discern the reality of the goodness of God's intentions and power to carry them out
- Prayer that creates conversation with God within biblical boundaries, freeing us from enslavement to old habitual patterns of thought, feeling, and action
- Worship that creates experience of the presence of God within biblical boundaries, allowing us to respond to God in spirit and in truth

A more objective approach, inspired by Glenn Daman in *Shepherding the Small Church*, is this list of criteria for the assessment of successful (fruitful) disciple-making:[17]

Spiritual maturity
1. Are people forming a Christian worldview?
2. Are prayer, Bible study, and worship regular disciplines in people's lives?
3. Are people obedient in acting responsibly in accordance with biblical principles?
4. Are people consistently putting God first with their time, talent, and treasure?

Personal piety
1. Are people dying to self-centeredness?
2. Are people demonstrating self-control?
3. Are people acting with kindness and patience toward others?
4. Are people denouncing self-promotion, personal privilege, and misuse of power?

Relational unity

1. Are people working through differences and disagreements?
2. Are people practicing forgiveness even (and especially) in hurtful relationships?
3. Are relationships being reconciled?
4. Are people knowing and being known, loving and being loved, serving and being served?

Missional integrity

1. Are people recognizing and ministering in their areas of giftedness?
2. Are people's gifts intentionally being used for mission in the world to serve and save the lost, as well as for maintenance of the church?
3. Are people taking on ministry responsibilities with accountability to a corporate focus on Christ-centered mission?
4. Are people performing all aspects of their ministries with humility, honesty, and honor?

All these work together for the glory of the Lord. For example, solitude prepares the way for study. It helps immeasurably to be freed up emotionally and fully prepared mentally to inquire into the things of the Lord. Study naturally leads to, and even requires, worship (as the following chapter describes). Willard clearly warns us, however, to remain diligent in our study: "We must not worship without study, for ignorant worship is of limited value and can be very dangerous. We may develop 'a zeal for God, but not according to knowledge' (Romans 10:2) and do great harm to ourselves and others."[18] We do well to heed this warning.

For Reflection and Discussion

1. How would you describe a disciple of Christ?
2. List the components of Jesus' command to his disciples in Matthew 28:19-20. Rate your church on a scale of one to ten with regard to all of the components.

3. It is possible to spend a lifetime studying the Bible and still miss the central theme. What is it? What should result from knowing it? (See John 5:39-40.)

4. What components would you expect to find in a Christian worldview?

5. The authors once parented an older foster child who would behave himself as long as an authority figure—parent, teacher, social worker—was nearby. Yet, he engaged in antisocial behavior apart from those people, even though he could quote the right expectations. Of what, from this chapter, would this be a picture?

6. What fruit would you look for in evaluating whether a student has learned to act responsibly in accordance with biblical principles?

7. Compare the advantages and disadvantages of the educational philosophy of separation by age and gender with those of the multigenerational, family context philosophy.

8. The teacher's responsibilities are to know the subject, make it interesting, and spur the student to responsible action. What are the student's responsibilities?

9. Sixteen assessment criteria for successful disciple-making were listed (p. 95-96). Which one(s) have been lacking in your own experience?

10. Having read this chapter, what items would you put on your "wish list" for your church home?

Getting Started

1. If your church were to make the successful completion of core courses a requirement for membership, what might those courses be that would help make mature disciples?

2. List eight to ten criteria that your church could initially consider to assess successful disciple-making.

3. Your church may not be ready for this one, but read through it and do what seems appropriate at this time. Ask your youth and adult teachers to attend a meeting to discuss building the Christian education program around making responsible decisions and making disciples. Give the following assignments:

   • Create age-level Christian worldviews using the five guidelines on page 86.

   • Discuss the relative merits of motivating student learning using external rewards and punishments and using internal consequences.

   • Share with one another how you see yourself and others in the room modeling for your students making responsible decisions.

   • Brainstorm how you might teach the application of biblical principles to a specific problem your students face. Use the six steps recommended by Wolterstorff (p. 89).

   • Evaluate each of your students using Wolterstorff's four criteria for evaluating student learning (p. 90).

8
worshiping

---

ideas for IMPROVING your church's ministry

26. Ten criteria for evaluating corporate worship
27. Three important questions to ask when choosing what songs to sing
28. Six questions for evaluating the purpose of the sermon
29. Four questions that put sermons to the ultimate test
30. Seven critical guidelines for the preacher to model with the sermon
31. Three important empirical conclusions for evaluating the necessity of regular sermons
32. Four criteria for genuine praise
33. Four steps for personally preparing for worship
34. Guidelines for implementing participatory worship services

---

Worship without study is dangerous. But study without worship is dangerous too. Dallas Willard makes a clear statement in *The Divine Conspiracy:*

Worship must be added to study to complete the renewal of our mind through a willing absorption in the radiant person who is worthy of all praise. Study without worship is ... dangerous.... To handle the things of God without worship is always to falsify them.[1]

When study and worship are disconnected, it opens the door to falsifying the things of God by "dumbing down" the substance of worship and even dumbing down God. Marva Dawn describes it well in *Reaching Out Without Dumbing Down:*[2]

- Dumbing down the substance of worship happens through preoccupation with the style of worship, for the purpose of attracting people rather than adoring God
- Dumbing down God himself happens by trivializing his person and marginalizing his presence

We want to portray in this chapter worship that lifts up the sacrifice of praise and bows down in humble adoration to an awesome God. This can best be done by maximizing the presence of the Holy Spirit through preoccupation with glorifying God by the worshiping community. Small churches have the advantage in this area: innovative worship with freedom to be truly participatory in creating genuine community worship.

Dumbing Down

What should a person do who is totally mystified after witnessing his first-ever baseball game? Go to another one. Similarly, what would you tell a person leaving your Sunday morning worship service, who says, "I didn't get it. It didn't make sense to me"? That happened several years ago after a chapel service at Yale University. Upon leaving, the story goes, a student approached the chaplain and said, "I didn't understand your message, and I don't understand Christianity." Whereupon the chaplain replied, "Come back next Sunday."

Without question, we want to welcome the stranger. However, we must not do so at the expense of the complexity within the simplicity of the gospel and the transcendence that coexists with the approachability of God. We must not buy into the modern trend of watering down everything "for dummies," putting *Worship for Dummies* right alongside *Baseball for Dummies.*

We must not allow dumbing down to steal the jewels of our worship services. The actual thieves that are stealing the jewels include the following ten. (The first five are drawn from Marva Dawn,[3] while six through ten are drawn from Ron Owens.[4])

1. Vicarious worship, or spectator worship
2. Worship that caters to narcissism, or self-centered worship
3. Market-driven worship, or worship determined by market analysis and marketing
4. Consumer-oriented worship, or worship geared more toward relevance than toward faithfulness
5. Success-oriented worship, or worship designed more for attracting the masses than for adoring the Master
6. Performance-oriented worship, or worship based more on the personality of the preacher than on the presence of God
7. Trivializing God, or replacing our acceptable worship of God with reverence and awe with chumminess and coziness
8. Reversing God's order, or focusing the worship service on people enjoying themselves rather than on God enjoying his people
9. Misusing God's name, or referring to God flippantly and irreverently in speech or song, or trying to manipulate God in prayer
10. Wrongly imaging God, or projecting a misguided or mistaken picture of who God is and what God is like to make him more palatable

Countless ways exist to dumb down worship. Many ways can also be found to prevent worship. One way to protect acceptable worship is to use these ten jewel thieves as criteria for evaluating your own worship services. You might also take a look at two components of the typical worship service that are particularly vulnerable to theft: singing and sermons.

Singing

We would like to share two observations about *what* we sing and *how* we sing as we gather together for worship. First, we become what we sing. Throughout the history of the Church, hymns have been a primary means of learning and expressing the fundamental doctrines of Christianity. Yet in recent years, the trend has been to switch to choruses in order to attract more people. Marva Dawn says the problem is that many modern praise choruses teach people to depend on their own feelings and efforts rather than on God's gift of grace. They are not so much about praising God, but about guiding people instead to consider how well they are loving him.[5]

The trend to de-emphasize hymns and replace them with choruses is seriously flawed. Dawn calls it "idolatrous" to assume that "if we choose the right *kind* of music people will be attracted to Christ. It is idolatry to think our work makes the difference. Christ himself draws people to believe in him through the Holy Spirit. Worship music is used to proclaim Christ, not to advertise him."[6] Our singing must carry the weight of the gospel, not the weight of public opinion.

What we sing is what we believe. Therefore, we must be careful about what we are teaching when we choose what we are going to sing. At The Gathering Church we blend a mixture of traditional and contemporary musical styles. In each case, we put it to the same test: Does it match up well against the ten criteria for evaluating corporate worship? Do the words reflect biblical accuracy? Can people sing the tune?

If we become what we sing, then one might conclude that we are becoming a bunch of adrenaline addicts. At least in some churches it would appear that way. We need to be aware of the deceptiveness of the rush of adrenalin that courses through our bodies when the entire congregation is whipped into a frenzy praising the Lord. We need to discern the difference between a mood-altering feeling of transcendence giving an adrenalin rush, and the presence of the Holy Spirit giving a true spiritual high.

If we recognize that our worship services can be scripted for excitement, with praise choruses following after each other, end-to-end without a pause, except for periodic mantra-like repetitions of key phrases, it should be evident that our emotions can be manipulated and we can become addicted to feelings in worship. This does not lead us to practice the presence of God. Similarly, when first-person pronouns dominate our singing, we should seriously consider the strong possibility that we are encountering our own feelings, rather than God.

That said, genuine worship involves the reality of our entire being. Our thoughts, emotions, and physical posture all bring glory to God when we worship God in spirit and in truth (John 4:24). Praise choruses inspire us to lift up our hands and voices in praise. Many hymns help us bow in humble adoration. Choruses and hymns are the warp and woof of acceptable worship, and they both must pass the same test.

Sermons

The music and the message are the two most prominent features of most modern worship services. In the typical service, the two most memorable activities are the people singing and the pastor "bringing the message," or preaching the sermon. The sermon, however, has become for many the focal point of the service. The sermon topic is often advertised, the service is frequently oriented toward the sermon, and the pastor and the service are usually evaluated based on the quality of the sermon. Therefore, let us turn our attention to the sermon's centrality.

The Centrality of the Sermon

The central importance of the sermon has drawn significant criticism through the years by such eminent critics as Dr. Charles Jefferson in the first quarter of the twentieth century. He thought it was wildly off the mark (even anathema) to consider preaching sermons the chief work and crowning function of the pastor. He was particularly upset with "pulpit-Pharaohs who are interested in building pyramids out of eloquent words."[7]

The drumbeat of discerning discontent has continued to this day. Following are some representative examples:

1. "The prime Sunday morning hour is viewed as a preaching service. Once the 'opening exercises' are dispensed with, everyone can concentrate on the high point, namely, the sermon," says J. Daniel Baumann.[8]

2. "Pastors ... have been thoroughly schooled in the erroneous belief that their main role is to preach. This false notion is a clear example of reading cultural trends into Scripture," says Bill Hull.[9]

3. "It is absurd to quote a New Testament statement that someone 'preached,' as though this clearly proved a regular Western-style preaching ministry," says David Norrington.[10]

This is not to say that sermons do not have or cannot have an important place in the worship service. But it does mean that the absolute, uncompromised focal point of the worship service must be divine presence and not human performance. William Hendricks's research into why people are leaving the church (as he reports in *Exit Interviews)* is relevant. When he asked them to describe their experiences with sermons, he found the following:

They were bored, but not necessarily because the preachers they heard were boring communicators. Some were rather brilliant. No, they were bored *spiritually*; they had no experience of God. The church service was just another meeting, the sermon just another harangue, no matter how well delivered. I don't know what you hope to accomplish with your preaching, but I do know why people ultimately go to church: they hope to find God there. They go for other reasons, too. But in the end, they're looking for God. So do they find Him in your sermons?[11]

All preachers must seek to answer that question. Are you in any way dumbing down your message? Are your sermons marked by simplistic formulations that marginalize the

Author of biblical truths? Are they "essentially 'McDoctrine'—spiritual fast-food of proof-texts and clichés that are filling and fattening, but not particularly nourishing?" asks Hendricks.[12] Does your desire to entertain and be liked invade your sermons? Or are you more concerned with content than with contentment, and are you willing to afflict the comfortable more than comfort the afflicted?

So what would God have us to do? The guidelines in Scripture that we applied to teaching in Chapter 7 can also be applied to preaching. In Ecclesiastes 12:10-11, the word *teacher* is used in some translations, while *preacher* is used in others. The preacher, therefore, should teach the plain truth and emphasize important truths in an interesting way, and spur people to action. As in teaching, the ultimate goal is responsible action. Hearers of the Word become responsible doers of the Word. Writes Dawn:

> *The ultimate test* (italics added) is whether sermons turn the hearers into theologians and activists. Do they grapple with texts and teach the people how to question? Do they wrestle with faith and invite the listeners to know that victory is assured? Do they struggle against the world's pain and challenge believers to create justice? Above all, do they bring us all into God's presence to hear his Word to us?[13]

As in teaching, modeling is a primary task. With some modification, this list from Dawn describes what preachers need to model:[14]

- How to unpack biblical texts
- How to think about God
- How to ask better questions
- How to raise theological issues about social ills
- How to apply biblical texts to real-life situations
- How to care for the poor and suffering
- How to teach attitudes and actions that listeners can apply to their own study and lives

The Effectiveness of the Sermon

If the ultimate goal of preaching is responsible action, then we must inquire into the effectiveness of the sermon. Do sermons change lives? Thirty years ago, Larry Richards came to the following conclusion, stated in *A New Face for the Church*, based on the findings of communications research:

> While the traditional sermon may potentially communicate blocks of information, the very form of this communication makes it difficult to receive feedback from listeners (to see if they have really understood what has been said, and its implications). More significant still, this form of communication has been shown most unlikely to change attitudes and values, and consequently, behavior. *Preaching seldom leads to whole-hearted response* (italics added).[15]

The Legitimacy of the Sermon

More recently, David Norrington has written *To Preach or Not to Preach?*, a thorough and massively documented (but not unwieldy) critique of the centrality, effectiveness, and even the legitimacy of the sermon. Among Norrington's conclusions are the following:

1. "In both Old and New Testament times ... sermons were delivered on special occasions or in order to deal with specific problems. The evidence suggests that they were not a common occurrence, as they are in almost all churches today."[16]
2. The regular use of the sermon has had two particularly important unintended harmful consequences. First, it frequently is ineffective, because the sermon/lecture is an inferior teaching method. Second, it fosters unhealthy dependence of the people on the pastor to study the Bible for them and to watch for and report on God's activity for them.[17]
3. "We are forced to ask how the use of the regular sermon today can be justified. One answer would be tradition.

But ... behind that tradition lies an even older tradition which knows nothing of regular sermons. This renders the argument from tradition difficult if not untenable."[18]

Tradition is not as good a basis for justifying the use of the regular sermon as is the more pragmatic consideration of whether it "works." Do sermons *work* in your church? Does the Holy Spirit work through your sermons to bring believers into God's presence so they may better know, love, and follow God? Do your sermons follow most if not all of the guidelines mentioned earlier?

What if the answer is that sermons are *not* working in your church? For example, what if you find that sermons mainly serve the status quo and cover for your church's failure in the areas of evangelism and education? What if you decide that the tradition of regular sermons in your church is broken? Should you try to fix it? Or should you consider the possibility that, as a wise person once said, "If it is not worth doing, it is not worth doing well"?

A large church, with multitudes in attendance on Sunday morning, will find it extremely difficult to consider giving the sermon a less prominent role or dropping it all together. However, the small church, with its greater freedom to innovate, has an advantage.

Fear not, little flock. This may be your opportunity to turn away from the "broken cistern" of the traditional sermon and return to "the spring of living water" for nourishment and renewal of your call to the uniqueness of your vision and ministry (Jeremiah 2:13).

Lifting Up and Bowing Down

The focal point of the worship service must be, unequivocally, our almighty and awesome God. None other is worthy of our praise. When you gather for worship, do you see God high and lifted up and hearts bowed before him?

Lifting up and bowing down—praise and worship—go together, but technically they are different. In his book titled *Worship,* Joseph Garlington asks us to "remember that while *praise* speaks of hands extended to God, *worship* speaks of bent knees and bowed faces pressed to the ground in [God's] awesome Presence."[19] These are two sides of the same coin.

Praise

When we *praise* the Lord, we often express appreciation for what God has done. Genuine praise, however, is more than appreciation. When we genuinely praise God, our spirit is lifted up in acknowledgment of who Jesus is. Genuine praise is adoring who Jesus is and acknowledging what he has done.

In other words, praising precious Jesus is more than our spirits being lifted up so that we can feel good again. It is more than singing an upbeat song so we can feel better about ourselves. Genuine praise focuses our spirit on our Redeemer. Jesus is the Light of the world, who brought us out of darkness. In our praise, he continues to take the darkness out of us. Our sacrifice of praise allows his light to shine and to challenge the darker realities within us.

Genuine praise is a discipline that forms and shapes us. Dawn writes, "[It] challenges our secularity and idolatries and narcissism by concentrating, not on our feelings of happiness, but on qualities in God that are truly there, not just there for me."[20] Genuine praise is also a discipline that dwells on God's all-sufficient fullness. This includes God's glory, grace, mercy, love, sovereignty, holiness, justice, power, immanence, transcendence, omnipresence, omniscience, mystery, goodness, and faithfulness. And more. Therein lies the power of praise.

Worship

When we *worship* the Lord, we should expect to enter into the discipline of practicing the presence of the Lord. Genuine worship, however, also includes fully entering into the discipline of participating in the work of the people.

Practicing the Presence of God

As we consider these two disciplines, we should take note of the need to prepare personally to enter into God's presence in worship. The first step is to confess Jesus Christ as Lord over our person and possessions. Second, we should be prepared to enter into God's presence with a "holy expectancy." We cultivate this sense that God will be powerfully present by living under the shadow of the Almighty, by practicing God's presence during the week. Everything we say and see and do is done with a listening ear for what God is saying and a watchful eye for what he is doing. Then as we enter the place of worship, we know that since we have heard God's voice throughout the week, we will be prepared to hear his voice in our worship together.

Third, we may want to pray a "trinitarian invocation":

- To repent, we can invoke the name of Jesus, perhaps by saying the "Jesus Prayer" that comes from the Orthodox tradition: "Lord Jesus Christ, Son of God, have mercy on me a sinner."
- To submit, we can invoke the promptings and power of the Holy Spirit, perhaps praying Psalm 143:10: "Teach me to do your will, for you are my God. May your gracious Spirit lead me forward on a firm footing."
- To abide, we wait on the Lord, perhaps praying Psalm 130:5 (Amplified): "I wait for [You] Lord, I expectantly wait, and in [Your] word do I hope."

Fourth, we need to remember that God has gathered us together as one body, in one accord, into his presence for his purpose.

Participating in the Work of the People

Practicing the presence of the Lord flows into and becomes part of the second discipline of worship, participating in the work of the people. "The work of the people" is the actual meaning of the word "liturgy," and unless the worshipers have no involvement at all, every worship service is "liturgical." Whether a service is liturgical or non-liturgical is not the important question. What matters is the degree to which worshipers take an active part in the worship service.

What is at stake is what Dawn refers to as "genuine 'community' worship—worship that is not the property of its leaders." She makes an impassioned plea: "Above all, the worship forms we use must foster 'the work of the people' and not be subject to the whims of the leaders. I cannot stress enough the requirement for worship to remain the people's work, the praise and prayer of the community gathered to offer itself as a living sacrifice."[21]

Years ago, Richards made a similar plea for "mutual ministry" as opposed to the more common services "in which the silent majority come to sit rather than to share." His plea was that every believer is "potentially a minister ... [and] a stimulator of the faith of others" and that "the entire New Testament concept of the church demands ... openness ... to permit the participation of any and every member. This is a principle which is basic, significant, and crucial in the renewal of the church."[22]

More than two decades later, Hendricks found that among people leaving the church, "perhaps the most common complaint was that worship services ... did little to help people meet God. However, I did not hear this as a call for more entertainment, but for more participation."[23]

When worshipers fully participate in worship, stimulating the faith of one another, they are truly participating in the work of the people. In *Real Worship*, Warren Wiersbe refers to these people as "transformers," participants who radiate the glory of God, as opposed to "conformers," spectators who merely reflect the glory of professional worship leaders and religious entertainers.[24]

Participatory Worship

When worshipers fully participate in the work of the people, God speaks *through* them as well as *to* them. In a truly participatory worship service, everyone comes with the expectation of contributing as the Holy Spirit leads. This does not at all mean that the service is disorderly, totally unplanned, and without leadership. God is not the author of confusion. Each church, however, must find its own level of comfort with preparation and structure, based on the spiritual discernment of the worship leaders, the spiritual maturity of the members and the spiritual giftedness of the entire body, all within the context of the church's particular heritage and tradition.

Worship at The Gathering is truly participatory, patterned after 1 Corinthians 14:26-33 and Colossians 3:16-17. We worship reverently and informally, sans sermon, giving everyone an opportunity to contribute: to sing, pray, teach, give a testimony, share what God has done in their lives recently, choose a hymn or chorus, or read from Scripture. Worship themes are announced in advance, but others often emerge as the Holy Spirit prompts and guides worshipers to share and express themselves. Themes may include, for example, attributes of God (sovereignty, holiness, goodness), a particular aspect of worship (prayer, praise, thanksgiving), or a basic biblical concept (redemption through Christ, lordship of Christ, comfort in Christ).

We are learning how to worship. With the diversity of backgrounds represented at The Gathering, it took us almost five years to get accustomed to participatory services. People who have been conditioned to be spectators in traditional-style worship services have had the most difficulty transitioning to a much more participatory style. We also have been hampered by the absence of skilled musical leadership. As pastoral leaders, we have needed a good deal of patience to leave control in God's hands and not automatically fill in "dead times" with what we have prepared ahead of time.

We do not intend to convey the idea that one particular biblical pattern has been established for all time and that everyone must follow it. God left plenty of room for flexible application of biblical principles across time and across cultures. Almost without exception, every worship service in our churches today is liturgical in the sense already discussed. Yet some definitely allow participation in the work of the people more than others.

How is your church doing? What might God say about your worship? Would his word be something like this, as Owens suggests?

> My people, when you gather to worship Me, do it in the nature of how I have revealed Myself to you in Scripture. It doesn't matter if the place where you meet is not aesthetically beautiful. Your pianist doesn't even have to play all the notes, and the choir doesn't have to sing all the harmonies perfectly. It doesn't matter if your group is small. You don't need spotlights, and you don't have to have a state-of-the-art sound system. You don't have to worry about appealing to the world with what you do, because when you worship Me in light of who I am, I will be with you and I will bless you.[25]

That is a wonderful promise indeed: "When you worship Me in light of who I am, [you don't have to fear, little flock, because] I will be with you and I will bless you."

For Reflection and Discussion

1. Both Dallas Willard and Marva Dawn are emphatic that studying about and knowing God are necessary if we are to be true worshipers. Describe the God you worship. Be as succinct as possible.

2. Why is it that in most churches, people usually critique the music and sermon?

3. Music can either help us worship God better or it can be perceived as trying to make God likable so people will be attracted to the worship service. What songs have helped you put God into your worship rather than yourself or your comfort?

4. If we "become what we sing," what are the people in your church becoming?

5. How has your church been robbed by one or more of the thieves that steal the jewels of worship?

6. People naturally want to feel the presence of the Lord while worshiping. What causes you to worship God even when that feeling is absent?

7. Sometimes churches try to make the worship service carry everything: evangelism, "bulletin board," entertainment, instruction, birthday and anniversary celebrations, and oh, yes ... worship. Would your church be open to the concept of focusing exclusively on God, on who he is and what he has done? What changes need to be made for this to happen?

8. Probably more "roast preacher" has been served on Sundays because of sermons (length, topic, delivery, accuracy) than any other reason. Given that sermons are usually lectures, and that is the least effective teaching method for the retention of material and lifestyle change, what other ways or means might be more effective to feed the flock?

9. Often the pastor feels an overwhelming responsibility to feed the flock through sermons, because he knows people do not get proper daily spiritual nourishment for various reasons. If the regular sermon were eliminated in your church, how long do you think you and others would survive spiritually?

10. What do you do during the week to practice the presence of the Lord? How could you improve in preparing for Sunday morning worship?

Getting Started

1. Task the leadership team with the following:
   - Evaluate your worship services using the ten criteria on page 101.
   - Put your corporate singing to the test using the three questions on page 102.
   - Put the pastor's sermons to the ultimate test (p. 105).
2. For the pastor:
   - Evaluate the purpose of your sermons using the four specific questions on page 105.
   - Evaluate your own presentation using the seven guidelines for what needs to be modeled with your sermons (p. 105).
   - What do you think you would personally lose or gain if you implemented participatory worship services using the guidelines on page 111?

9

praying

---

ideas for IMPROVING your church's ministry

Some people say praying is intimidating. Others say praying seems empty and useless. A good many people see prayer as just a routine "church thing."

On the positive side, there are countless churchgoers who want prayer to "work" for them. They have a deep desire to draw closer to God and see God at work in their lives. They want to learn how to pray, live fruitful lives, and be empowered in their walk with the Lord. The prayer Dutch Sheets gives in *Intercessory Prayer* may well be theirs: "We are tired of cloaking our ignorance in robes of blind obedience and calling it spirituality. We are tired of religious exercises that make us feel better for a while but bear little lasting fruit. We are tired of a form of godliness without the power."[1]

Discontent with spiritual mediocrity is an expression of hope. It says, "I want to grow and I want a church where I can." The environment we have created at The Gathering Church is an intentional response to that sentiment. Praying is foundational to everything we do. We have articulated (below) the values (a) and practices (b) that determine the seven standards that guide our prayer ministries:

1. Mission
   a. God loves us, and our mission is to show our love for God through obedience.
   b. We minister through prayer in obedience and in agreement with God's loving purposes.

2. Model
   a. Jesus Christ is our foundation and model.
   b. We minister through prayer because of Christ's example and invitation and in a Christlike manner.

3. Means
   a. The Holy Spirit is God's empowering presence within us.
   b. We minister through prayer in the power of the Spirit.

4. Measure
   a. The Bible is the ultimate measure of our Christian faith and practice.
   b. We minister through prayer under the guidance of Scripture.

5. Medium
   a. The Church is Christ's chosen instrument to implement God's kingdom—already here and not yet fully revealed.
   b. We minister through prayer as members of one body— the Church universal in all its particular expressions.

6. Motive
   a. Love is our motive.
   b. We minister through prayer with compassion for other people and respect for their dignity and freedom of choice.

7. Method
   a. Corporate, conversational prayer is the preferred form.
   b. We minister through prayer in one accord to claim victory in Christ and enforce the victory of light over darkness.

The purpose of prayer at The Gathering is to know God's purposes and pray them back to God. We are learning how to pray and are seeing amazing results. God is showing us how to work with him. Productive, praying people have always known what we have discovered for ourselves. One voice in particular stands out—that of S. D. Gordon:

Prayer surely does influence God. It does not influence his purpose. It does influence his action. Everything that ever has been prayed for, of course I mean every right thing, God has already purposed to do. But ... he has been hindered in his purposes by our lack of willingness. When we learn his purposes and make them our prayers we are giving him the opportunity to act.[2]

The primary work of the church is to pray. We agree together, in harmony with God's purposes, to release the power of the Holy Spirit to claim the victory we have in Christ and enforce the victory of light over darkness. Small churches have the advantage in making prayer foundational for everything the church does, while establishing corporate prayer as the cornerstone of the church as a house of prayer.

Agreeing in One Accord
House of Prayer

Jesus said, "My house shall be called a house of prayer" (Matthew 21:13; also, Isaiah 56:7; Luke 19:46). It is not a house of great sermons or music or even people, but a house of prayer. A house of prayer is not just a church that prays, but a church that is devoted to prayer. The following differences from Fred Hartley's article in *Pray!* magazine are telling:

A Church that Prays	A Church Devoted to Prayer
1. Prays about what it does.	1. Does things by prayer.
2. Fits prayer in.	2. Gives prayer priority.
3. Prays when there are problems.	3. Prays when there are opportunities.
4. Announces a special time of prayer and some people in the church show up.	4. Announces a special time of prayer and the church shows up.
5. Asks God to bless what it is doing.	5. Asks God to enable it to do what he is blessing.
6. When faced with financial shortfall, backs down from projects.	6. When challenged by financial shortfall, calls for fasting, prayer, and faith.
7. Is tired, weary, stressed out.	7. Mounts up with wings like eagles, runs and does not grow weary, walks and does not faint.
8. Does things within its means.	8. Does things beyond its means.
9. Sees its members as its parish.	9. Sees the world as its parish.
10. Is involved in human work.	10. Is involved in God's work.[3]

A house of prayer does not ask God to bless what it is doing. It asks God to enable it to do what he is blessing!

Corporate Prayer

The people in a house of prayer pray together often. At The Gathering, we have corporate prayer three times a week: Wednesday and Saturday evenings for an hour and a half and Sunday mornings for half an hour. We have found an undeniable link between corporate prayer and answered prayer. A number of situations of deep personal concern to individuals and families in our congregation were prayed for privately over the course of several years without an answer. Then these concerns were brought to corporate prayer and something changed. The prayers were answered! What changed was the exponential power of corporate prayer.

Just because people meet together does not mean power is added to prayer. One person may pray for a whole list of things and everyone says "Amen," but often only that one person is praying. God desires hearts in agreement, not just our "amens" in unison. Praying with agreeing hearts is praying in one accord, as in Acts 4:24 when the believers were united as they lifted their voices in prayer. Audible, conversational sharing of burdens and our desire to want what God wants guide our corporate prayer.

In *With Christ in the School of Prayer*, Andrew Murray lists three excellent guidelines for ensuring that prayer is effectual:[4]

1. We agree not merely with what others may ask, and together desire it, but we are distinctly united in spirit and in truth.
2. We gather in Jesus' name, where he is the center of our corporate union.
3. We expect answered prayer, the fruit of our endeavor.

Prayer Styles

Unfortunately, some people at corporate prayer gatherings may confuse unity with uniformity. Some will think that everyone must pray in the same way, using the same language, tone of voice, and even posture. They believe in sameness of behavior rather than oneness in spirit.

Prayer meetings can benefit from differing prayer styles. Different styles arise from differences in personality, plus different spiritual gifts. We need to capitalize on that fact, because God wants our hearts, not a bunch of clones. Alice Smith in a *Pray!* magazine article provides good examples of spiritual-gifts based intercessory prayer styles:[5]

1. Flexible intercessors have the gift of discernment and pray as the Holy Spirit leads.

2. Crisis intercessors have gifts of prophecy, mercy, faith, healing, pastoral care, or service, and "they sense the urgency in every situation."

3. Intercessors for the nations are gifted with a mix of evangelism, prophecy, faith, and mercy, and "they stand in the gap for the nations of the world."

4. Mercy-motivated intercessors have gifts of mercy, healing, faith, giving, and helping, and "they pray with compassion and empathy and can minister to heartaches with encouragement and love."

5. Prayer-list intercessors have gifts of administration or teaching, and "their priority is to persevere for the people, places, and issues on their prayer lists."

6. Prophetic intercessors tend toward prophecy, exhortation, faith, wisdom, word of knowledge, and discernment, and they are able to hear from God as he "shares his heart and the strategies of his work with them."

7. Special-assignment intercessors have pastoral gifts and shepherding hearts, and "their primary concern is to protect and care for the body of Christ."

8. Warfare intercessors, gifted with a mix of revelatory gifts of faith, wisdom, word of knowledge, discernment of spirits, or prophecy, are poised so that "when the Lord reveals enemy targets, these warriors will lock in and release a payload of prayer."

9. Administrative intercessors have gifts of leadership, giving, exhortation, faith, and administration, so they are good coordinators and facilitators who keep things moving along.

Hindrances

Prayer styles are primarily suggestive but also illustrative of the richness of the prayer meetings where the Holy Spirit is freely moving. That said, the Holy Spirit may also be hindered in corporate praying. In *The Praying Church,* Sue Curran lists common hindrances, including:[6]

1. Teaching prayers: making a point or giving information that is "too valuable" to keep to oneself, spilling one's mind over to people rather than pouring out one's heart to God
2. Controlling prayers: bringing the group under the direction of a self-appointed leader
3. Doctrinal or attitudinal prayers: correcting the doctrine or intention of others
4. Emotional prayers: unburdening one's feelings at the gathering's expense
5. Morbid, unbelieving prayers: expressing fear or depression or unbelief without asking for God's intervention
6. Intellectual prayers: performing rehearsed prayers or, as G. Campbell Morgan put it, "giving the Almighty information of which he had been in possession long before the man was born"[7]
7. Dead prayers: praying from habit rather than inspiration
8. Personal, ambitious prayers: praying "to be heard, to maintain [one's] public image, or to impress the hearers with [one's] potential for future leadership"
9. Uncooperative prayers: being a "lone ranger," with an unteachable spirit and lack of sensitivity toward others

We would add to the list "prayerless prayers," from the unparalleled words of E. M. Bounds in *Purpose in Prayer:*

Prayerless praying ... is not based on desire, and is devoid of earnestness and faith. Desire burdens the chariot of prayer, and faith drives its wheels. Prayerless praying has no burden.... Prayerless praying stakes nothing on the issue, for it has nothing to stake. It comes with empty hands.... Prayerless praying has no heart in its praying. The lack of heart deprives praying of its reality, and makes it an empty and unfit vessel.... Prayerless praying is insincere. It has no honesty at heart. We name in words what we do not want in heart.... [I] once heard an eminent and saintly preacher ... come abruptly and sharply on a congregation that had just risen from prayer, with the question and statement, "What did you pray for? If God should take hold of you and shake you, and demand what you prayed for, you could not tell him to save your life what the prayer was that has just died from your lips."

So it always is, prayerless praying has neither memory nor heart. A mere form, a heterogeneous mass, an insipid compound, a mixture thrown together for sound and to fill up, but with neither heart nor aim, is prayerless praying. A dry routine, a dreary drudge, a dull and heavy task is this prayerless praying.[8]

Conversational Prayer

At The Gathering we have found that an excellent way to prevent some of these hindrances to corporate praying is through modeling that naturally takes place during the conversational method of prayer. We keep the guidelines for conversational prayer simple, which makes modeling easy:

1. Start by praising God.
2. Speak loudly enough for others to hear.
3. Be brief.
4. Pray your requests and give thanks instead of taking "prayer requests."
5. Focus on one topic at a time.
6. Others join in, if so led, before moving on.
7. As in conversation, feel free to pray more than once.

Our main concern is that while we do well to recognize that one's individual manner of praying may be a disruption of unity and hindrance to effectual prayer, we must not restrict the work of the Holy Spirit. Conversational prayer is the best method we know of for not silencing the very voice or voices the Lord wants to use. We must not quench the Spirit!

Claiming and Enforcing Victory
Intercessory Prayer

Corporate intercessory prayer has three parts: (1) *agreement* (every heart is united); (2) *accumulation* (every voice is heard); and (3) *activation* (power is released). We have been discussing agreement and now turn to accumulation and activation.

A wonderful picture of the accumulation of our prayers of intercession shows up in Revelation 5:8, describing "golden bowls full of incense, which are the prayers of the saints." These prayers are not the vain repetitions of functionaries or the litanies of "holy men," as though filling the golden bowls is just a matter of accumulating words, cold-hearted words. No, these prayers are the individual and corporate cries from the heart of all the saints.

However, two things are noteworthy. First, not all the prayers of all the saints will necessarily reach the golden bowls. In *Prayer Is Invading the Impossible*, Jack Hayford lists prayers that fail to reach their goal:

1. Prayers of self-indulgence will not be answered (James 4:2-3).
2. Presumptuous attitudes in prayer will not be honored (Luke 9:51-56).
3. Prayer offered from a heart that simultaneously calculates disobedience will not even be heard (Psalm 66:18).
4. Mouthing prayer while tolerating unforgiveness toward others blocks the provision of even our most basic needs (Matthew 6:11-12).[9]

Second, not all effective prayer must take a long time. The need for prayers to accumulate does not necessarily mean it has to take "forever." When both the filling of bowls in Revelation 5:8 and the releasing of power in Revelation 8:3-5 are considered, Dutch Sheets says, "God has something in which he stores our prayers for use at the proper time.... According to these verses, either when he knows it is the right time to do something or when enough prayer has accumulated to get the job done, he releases power."[10]

What power it is! Charles Spurgeon gives an awesome picture of the pouring out of power from the heavenlies in *The Power of Prayer in a Believer's Life*:

> Then will come voices—preachers here and there rise, voices denouncing oppression, voices crying against false religion, voices preaching truth, voices declaring Christ. Then will come thunderings, for with the Gospel will go the voice of God, which thunders louder than the voices of [humans]. Then will flash forth lightnings, for the light of God's power and truth will come forth with majesty, and [people's] hearts shall be smitten with it and made obedient to it. And then shall earthquakes shake society, till the thrones of despots reel, till hoary customs are dashed in pieces, till the land that could not be plowed with the Gospel shall be broken up with the secret heavings from the Eternal God.[11]

The activation of the release of power is what intercessory prayer is all about. God's people cry out in one accord, wanting what God wants. Their prayers accumulate. Then God releases voices denouncing oppression and declaring Christ. He releases thunderings of the gospel louder than human voices, flashes the light of his power and truth into human hearts, and shakes sinful society "with the secret heavings from the Eternal God." All this is done with a singular purpose: reclaiming that which rightfully belongs to Jesus.

The adversary has invaded God's boundaries, and the church prays to shake those areas of captivity free from Satan's control. Intercessory prayer is God's provision for reestablishing divinely intended boundaries. Our task is to invade the impossible, by praying boldly and confidently until we have grown into our inheritance of peace and prosperity and the boundary lines have fallen in pleasant places (Psalm 18:17-19; Psalm 16:6).

It is almost inconceivable that God needs our prayers. Yet he does! In Dutch Sheets's words:

> God has chosen to work through people.... Though God is sovereign and all-powerful, Scripture clearly tells us that He limited Himself, concerning the affairs of earth, to working through human beings.... How many promises from God have gone unfulfilled because He can't find the human involvement He needs? ... God *needs* our prayers.[12]

For us to fully understand what we are to do, we must first understand what God has already accomplished. In a word, it is done: The *work* of intercession is already done. Jesus interceded "between God and humanity, reconciling us to the Father; and between Satan and humanity, breaking Satan's hold," says Sheets.[13] That was the finished work of the cross. Jesus has won the victory over sin and Satan.

The *prayer* of intercession is what we do. According to Sheets, our intercessory prayers create a meeting with God for the purpose of asking him to meet with specific people to communicate to them his reconciling love through Jesus Christ. Or, our intercessory prayers create a meeting with satanic forces of opposition for the purpose of undoing their diabolical meetings with specific people, by confronting the powers of darkness with the victory of Calvary. This is what we do: We bring Christ's salvation and break Satan's strongholds. We claim victory in Jesus (death to sin) and enforce the victory of light over darkness (defeat of Satan).

Praying for the Community

Satan and his forces can be corporately addressed in various ways to reclaim the territory, both material and immaterial, they have stolen. Peter Wagner mentions three in *Churches That Pray*.[14] First, he mentions concerts of prayer. These are an attempt to combine praying for revival in the church and outreach in the community.[15] Second are prayer summits, which are concerned with renewal and unity among the pastors of the churches in the community.[16] A third way is prayerwalking, which focuses on neighborhoods. It is on-site prayer, while walking through the neighborhood, making contact with the people for whom prayers are being said. Prayerwalking has a long history and has made a significant impact for the cause of Christ.[17]

Fasting

Fasting prepares the soil for inspired prayer that bears the fruit of releasing God's power from the heavenlies to where it is needed on earth. Where power is most needed determines the prayer focus that in turn determines when fasting is most needed.

Like study, worship, and prayer, fasting can and should be done both individually and corporately. In *Fasting for Spiritual Breakthrough*, Elmer Towns counsels, "A private problem requires a private fast. A group problem requires the group to fast.... Even when the circle of concern becomes national, the circle of fasting should be as large as the circle of concern."[18] That is good advice: the circle of fasting (and praying too!) should be as large as the circle of concern.

Corporate fasting in combination with corporate praying can be a powerful and unifying experience. Towns cautions, however, that some people get the idea that their "good works" earn answered prayer. That idea is clearly incorrect. Towns writes that "the power of fasting to bring people closer to God [and to one another] resides in God, not in the 'work' of fasting. The outer work of fasting can reflect the inner heart's desire, but it is not a work of human effort that binds God to respond (see Isaiah 58:1-5). In His sovereignty, God sees the heart and responds."[19] Towns provides many biblical, practical guidelines, and examples for understanding and practicing fasting in a productive and healthful manner.

Richard Foster also offers helpful and succinct cautions and encouragements regarding fasting in his classic book *Celebration of Discipline:*

1. Fasting requires that we center on God. "Every other purpose must be subservient to God.... Physical benefits, success in prayer, the enduing with power, spiritual insights—these must never replace God as the center of our fasting."[20]

2. Fasting reveals "the things that control us.... We cover up what is inside us with food and other good things, but in fasting these things surface. If pride controls us, it will be revealed almost immediately. David writes, 'I humbled my soul with fasting' (Psalm 69:10). Anger, bitterness, jealousy, strife, fear—if they are within us, they will surface during fasting."[21]

3. Fasting reminds us that "food does not sustain us; God sustains us.... Fasting is feasting [on the things of the Lord]!"[22]

4. Fasting rewards us with freedom from the nonessentials of life. "Our human cravings and desires are like rivers that tend to overflow their banks; fasting helps keep them in their proper channels.... Numerous people have written on the many other values of fasting such as increased effectiveness in intercessory prayer, guidance in decisions, increased concentration, deliverance for those in bondage, physical well-being, revelations, and so on.

In this, as in all matters, we can expect God to reward those who diligently seek him."[23]

When we step back from the details of intercessory prayer and fasting, let us not be overcome by fear of being totally defeated by a defeated enemy. Let us not expend all our energy cursing the darkness of the world rather than shining the light of the Word. Hayford puts this into perspective:

In honor of His own Son who died to make possible the full invasion of His almighty power into the impossibilities of earth, God will do nothing apart from the people His Son has redeemed. Jesus urged that we pray for the entrance of the Father's kingdom power in all situations. He urged that we not succumb to the fears that argue for surrender to earth or hell's worst ... or their least. We are simply not to tolerate that which diminishes, demeans, distresses or destroys. *Instead:* "Seek first God's kingdom, and all these things shall become a plus!" [and] "Don't be afraid, little flock, it is the Father's delight to make a gift to you of His overruling power."(See Luke 12:31, 32)[24]

For Reflection and Discussion

1. By its actions, would you say your church is a church that prays or a church that is devoted to prayer? Document your answer.

2. What does S. D. Gordon mean when he says, "Prayer surely does influence God. It does not influence His purpose. It does influence His action"?

3. It is not unusual for people to protest the need to meet together for prayer, saying they "can pray at home." What are some strengths of praying together? What things have kept you from praying with others?

4. Name two specific things you learned from the examples of prayer styles given by Alice Smith (p.120).

5. Which hindrance(s) to corporate praying have you identified in others? in yourself?
6. Why do you think God often takes a long time to answer prayers?
7. People frequently ask why they should bother to pray, since God is sovereign. How would you answer that?
8. Reread the description of Peter Wagner's ideas about prayerwalking (p. 126). With whom would you like to do this? How will you suggest it to the person(s) who came to mind?
9. A number of cautions and encouragements are given regarding fasting (p. 126–128). Did you find yourself skimming or skipping this section because you did not think it applied to you? Go back and read it again and see how God might be speaking to you.
10. Taking "prayer requests" can eat up a lot of precious prayer time. How can conversational prayer address both the need for enough information to pray intelligently and the need to use the entire time for prayer?

Getting Started

1. Consider holding weekly corporate conversational prayer meetings. Try it without taking prayer requests, while holding to the guidelines on page 122. Give it time to work.
2. Rather than meeting in a building for prayer, some people prefer active prayerwalking. Form a team of no more than six people:
   • Pray for God's leading for your choice of a neighborhood to visit.
   • Before going, spend time in prayer to prepare your hearts and ask the Holy Spirit to prepare the soil.
   • Grow into this ministry! Limit your first time out to no

more than half an hour, and increase it when the team starts asking for more.

- Walk together slowly up one side of the block or road and back down the other, praying with your eyes open for what God may show you.

- As you return to pray at various times, your team may become a familiar sight. Look for opportunities to pray for individuals and their specific situations.

3. If you have never fasted before, do not attempt a forty-day fast! Start with a partial fast—perhaps one day a week. Seek the Lord's guidance in deciding why you should do this and how he would like to use this spiritual discipline to further his kingdom.

10

giving

---

ideas for IMPROVING your church's ministry

Billy Graham says, "Tell me what you think about money, and I can tell you what you think about God."[1] Graham has taken his cue from Luke 16:11, where Jesus asks essentially how those who cannot properly handle money can be entrusted with true riches. The implication is clear: How can you be entrusted with spiritual responsibilities? How can your church be entrusted with souls?

Good stewardship is the biblical requirement for true riches. It is the prerequisite for effective evangelism and discipling ministries. It is foundational for every other ministry as well. Every church that desires effective ministries must properly handle its money, which includes giving unselfishly for the good of others and for the advancement of God's kingdom.

Good stewardship is living generously and simply, individually and corporately, always remembering to put God first. Once again, the small church has the advantage in creating stewardship structures that eliminate the *pressure* on giving and encourage the *pleasure* of giving, while adjusting its corporate lifestyle to become a biblically faithful, giving community.

Giving Spirit

Jesus said: "If you only love the lovable, do you expect a pat on the back? Run-of-the-mill sinners do that. If you only help those who help you, do you expect a medal? Garden-variety sinners do that. If you only give for what you hope to get out of it, do you think that's charity? The stingiest of pawnbrokers does that," (Luke 6:32-34, *The Message)*.

Giving for what they hope to get in return is not even the first option for many people. We repeatedly hear people say, "I can't afford to give." Period. End of discussion. As disciples of Jesus— citizens of the kingdom—we cannot afford *not* to give! Rather than asking, "What can I spare?" the kingdom-conscious question is, "What can I share?" That comes from a giving spirit.

Good Stewardship

The mark of a giving spirit is giving to God first, which is also the mark of being a good steward (Deuteronomy 14:23, TLB). Stewardship is a broadly defined concept, but it does have some definite characteristics such as ones Jack Hayford names in *The Spirit-Formed Church:*[2]

- Awareness of God's claim on our time, talents, and treasure
- Faith in God's covenant of blessing upon obedient stewards
- Giving tithes and offerings
- Joy that releases this spirit of sacrifice

In other words, biblical stewardship entails putting God first with our time, talents, and treasure. It involves believing God will bless our obedience, practicing the covenant privilege of tithing (see Chapter 5), and portraying a sacrificial, giving spirit released by the joy of responding to *God's* generosity in making *us* channels of blessings.

The joy of sacrifice—at least for others—is a foreign idea in our affluent society. One would expect an increase in wealth to lead to a proportionate increase in giving, but that simply is not the case. People in the United States worship the unholy trinity of individualism, materialism, and consumerism. Our allegiance is to ourselves and what we can get, not what we can give. A cartoon caption in the *Seattle Post-Intelligencer* a few years ago says it perfectly:

I pledge allegiance to myself
and the goodies I get from America,
and to all the money for which I hustle,
one person, lookin' good, irresponsible,
with profit and pleasure above all!

People forfeit nearness to God by running after material gain. In *Rich Christians in an Age of Hunger,* Ron Sider writes, "Modern people have lost the biblical sense of human limitations. We want more and more faster and faster.... God's Word is strikingly different: 'Do not wear yourself out to get rich; have the wisdom to show restraint' (Proverbs 23:4)."[3] In his call to move from affluence to generosity, Sider bluntly challenges our idolatry:

It is idolatrous nonsense to suggest that human fulfillment comes from an ever-increasing supply of material things.... We must redefine the good life.... We must develop models of simpler lifestyles; corporate policies that permit people to choose parenting, leisure, and community service over maximizing income and profits; and ... advertising practices that discourage overconsumption.[4]

Simple Living

A good place to begin considering the possibility of simpler lifestyles is to review the following symptoms of the modern-day plague called "affluenza," taken from a guide distributed by KCTS Television in Seattle, Washington:

1. Shopping fever
   - On average, Americans shop six hours a week and spend only 40 minutes playing with their children.
   - What is the lure of shopping and material possessions?
2. Chronic stress
   - "We hear the same refrain all the time from people. 'I have no life.... I get home at night, there's laundry, bills to pay.... I'm exhausted, I go to sleep, I wake up and the routine begins the next day all over again,'" says Gerald Celente of the Trends Research Institute.
   - How has this work-spend treadmill affected the quality of life for you and your loved ones?
3. Hypercommercialism
   - By the age of 20, the average American has seen a million commercials. Advertising accounts for two-thirds of the space in our newspapers and 40 percent of our mail.
   - How does advertising influence your life and personal buying habits?
4. A rash of bankruptcies
   - In 1997, more than 1.1 million Americans declared personal bankruptcy, more than those who graduated from college.
   - How have credit cards made it possible for us to spend beyond our means?
5. Fractured families
   - In 90 percent of divorce cases, arguments about money play a prominent role.
   - How do materialism and other money issues create conflict in your family?

6. Social scars
   • The gap between the rich and poor in the United States is the widest in any developed nation.
   • How does "affluenza" contribute to this gap?
7. Resource exhaustion
   • Since 1950, Americans have used more resources than everyone who ever lived before them.
   • How can we encourage corporations to produce more environmentally sound goods and services?[5]

For those who have begun moving from affluence to generosity in their thinking and who want to move to simplicity in their living, the symptoms of affluenza are persuasive reasons for doing so. The following list was developed from "An Evangelical Commitment to Simple Lifestyle," written in response to the resolve expressed in the Lausanne Covenant of 1974 to "develop a simple lifestyle."[6]

1. Honor God as the owner of all things.
2. Manage on less and give away more.
3. Renounce waste and oppose extravagance.
4. Denounce hoarding and building "bigger barns."
5. Denounce environmental destruction.
6. Distinguish between necessities and luxuries.
7. Distinguish between modesty and vanity.
8. Distinguish between commitment to quality and slavery to fashion.
9. Distinguish between creative hobbies and empty status symbols.
10. Distinguish between occasional celebrations and frequent overindulgence.
11. Relieve the needs of less privileged believers.
12. Seek justice and relief for the poor who are exploited and powerless to defend themselves.

We believe the major problem in getting from "What can I spare?" to "What can I share?" is the struggle with making sure that we have enough and trusting God to provide for our needs. Obedience is the fundamental issue.

The manna story in Exodus 16 is forcefully instructive about the nature of God's provision. First, we learn not to hoard. Anything that is hoarded rots. What do we hold onto that is excess when others are in need? Second, we learn that God's provision requires obedience. And we know that is not easy. As Christians, we may yet find ourselves in a similar position to the nation of Israel during the wilderness years, having come out of Egypt (as we have, Romans 6), into the wilderness (as we have, Romans 7), but not yet arriving in Canaan (as we have not if we have not fully trusted God and entered into his rest, Romans 8). By trusting in God and yielding to his provision through Jesus Christ, we have been delivered from bondage to human provision. However, we must pass through the wilderness of learning to rely more perfectly on God's provision.

Redemption is not full emancipation all at once. Complete freedom to rely fully on Christ's provision is a lifelong journey of faith. In *The Saving Life of Christ*, Major Ian Thomas says "Forty weary years it took before God was able, through Joshua, to teach his people that to *get in* takes precisely the same kind of faith that it takes to *get out*—the faith that trusts God and says, 'Thank you'!"[7]

Paul refers to Exodus 16:18 in 2 Corinthians 8:12-15 when he speaks of how obedient giving results in everyone experiencing God's provision. Paul's word to both the giver and the receiver are encouraging:

> If you are really eager to give, it isn't important how much you are able to give. God wants you to give what you have, not what you don't have. Of course, I don't mean you should give so much that you suffer from having too little. I only mean that there should be some equality. Right now you have plenty and can help them. Then at some

other time they can share with you when you need it. In this way, everyone's needs will be met. Do you remember what the Scriptures say about this? "Those who gathered a lot had nothing left over, and those who gathered only a little had enough."

What a giving spirit! What a giving community!

Giving Community

The mentality of a giving spirit permeates the entire lifestyle of the obedient Christian. The same should be true of the body of Christ. Obedient churches are giving communities with corporate lifestyles that reflect Christ's presence on earth.

In *Enough Is Enough,* Bishop John Taylor challenges churches to "stop trying to keep up with the ecclesiastical Joneses in ... apparatus and techniques and go for simplicity of means in our mission." Let us not, "like King Saul of old, put [our] trust in heavy accoutrements and expensive weapons. He could not bear to see the shepherd boy going unarmed into the contest with Goliath, and almost smothered him with equipment. But David knew better."[8]

Does your church know better? Check your church budget. The statement, "Show me your checkbook, and I'll show you where your heart is," applies equally well to churches and individuals. Do not be surprised if you find that your church has allowed its thought and its action to be shaped by the values and preferences of our affluent, materialistic society. Do not be surprised if your church puts its trust in an elaborate corporate lifestyle and is preparing itself for battle by being smothered with equipment.

The Gathering Church has worked hard to meet Bishop Taylor's challenge. We definitely "go for simplicity of means in our mission." We most definitely do not smother ourselves with equipment. From the first day, we have not allowed our operating needs to hold hostage our giving to missions. We will not collect, budget, or disburse funds to support an extravagant corporate lifestyle. This becomes clear when we examine how we collect tithes and offerings, budget after the fact, give to the poor and to the Jewish people, and pay the pastor's compensation.

Collecting Tithes and Offerings

We do not "beat people up" to get their money so we can "keep up with the ecclesiastical Joneses." We follow two explicit guidelines to prevent that. The first is that we never ask for money, take pledges, or pass the plate. And we have committed ourselves to being a true faith ministry from the beginning and onward. Our goal is to be a healthy church, where the people have a willing heart and a generous spirit.

Our desire is to decrease the *pressure* on giving and increase the *pleasure* of giving. Our inspiration comes from Scripture: "The Lord said to Moses, 'Tell the people of Israel that every one who wants to may bring me an offering'" (Exodus 25:1-2). Then "everyone who was willing and whose heart moved him came and brought an offering to the Lord" (Exodus 35:21, NIV). Furthermore, 2 Corinthians 9:7 says, "Every one must make up his own mind as to how much he should give. Don't force anyone to give more than he really wants to, for cheerful givers are the ones God prizes" (TLB).

Our second guideline is to make the opportunity to give unobtrusive but obvious. Near the entrance to the worship area we have placed a clearly labeled tithes and offerings box, inspired by the Old Testament account of collecting contributions for temple repairs in a large chest with a hole in the lid. When the chest became full, two people other than the king (the king's financial secretary being one) counted and took care of the money (2 Kings

12: 6-12). We follow this procedure each week with our financial secretary and a second person from a rotating pool of trustworthy adults.

Visitors to The Gathering frequently mention how relieved they are not to be confronted with an offering plate passing under their nose and how pleased they are to discover the offering box on their own. Many people who attend regularly say how pleased they are that we are not like so many other churches that are "always asking for money." Little children gleefully look for big people to hoist them up so they can drop their coins into the box.

Budgeting After the Fact

Another unconventional feature of our system for handling money is that we budget "after the fact." That means that we distribute all the undesignated funds received the previous month. If much came in, much goes out; if little came in, little goes out.

We begin the budgeting process by drawing "splits" for the coming year at the annual meeting. The splits are in two categories: giving and operating. They are the percentages for distributing all of the undesignated funds received during the previous month. The splits range from 70/30 giving/operating to 30/70 giving/operating, with five percent increments. Our very first year, before we had created the present system, we adopted a split of 75/25. For the following years the giving/operating split has been 70/30 twice, 65/35 three times, 60/40 once, 55/45 once and 50/50 once. We had a reversal of the priority of giving over operating only once: 30/70. For our first ten years, The Gathering has averaged a giving percentage of slightly greater than 60 percent, as the Lord has led.

On the last Sunday of each month, we determine where the funds in the giving category will be distributed. We have two containers: one for the "Mission of the Month" and the other for the "Needy of the Month." There are presently twenty-six old sewing thread spools in the Mission of the Month container representing missionaries, Bible distribution, prison ministry, medical aid, relief and development, aid for orphans, radio broadcasting, and other ministries. These are all effective ministries operating in Africa, Asia, Europe, and Latin America, as well as in the United States.

There are five spools in the Needy of the Month container representing groups that serve in western Washington, such as the local food bank, Pregnancy Resource Service, and Union Gospel Mission in Seattle. A sixth spool is for local needs. The recipient of our giving to local needs is determined by the Core Group from needs of which they have been made aware. They may be needs either inside or outside the congregation. Perhaps someone needs help to pay a propane bill, buy car tires, or pay for counseling for a sexually abused child.

To determine the distributions, someone first prays for God's guidance and blessing. Then one of the children shakes the Mission of the Month container and takes it to an adult who reaches in, pulls out a spool, reads what is written on it, and then returns it to the container. The same procedure is repeated with the Needy of the Month container.

God knows the needs of the individuals and groups whose names are in our containers. We trust God also knows how much will be given during the coming month and that God will match the amount to the need. People look forward each month to see what God is going to do. They get excited when an individual or group that they have a strong personal interest in gets drawn. They also are so pleased when they hear a report of the timeliness of their giving: "How did you know about our unexpected need?" or "It couldn't have happened without your substantial gift." Never before have we been in a church where people are eager to see where they get to give their money!

Giving to the Poor and to the Jewish People

We have a special interest in giving to the poor and to ministries that reach Jewish people. Scripture clearly presents God as caring for the poor and says that our giving to the poor honors God (Proverbs 14:31). In addition, God has never rescinded the promise to Abraham: "I will bless those who bless you and curse those who curse you" (Genesis 12:3). The gospel is the power of God at work, saving all who believe. And God enjoins us specifically to proclaim the gospel among the Jewish people (Romans 1:16; 10:14). Therefore, in addition to giving monthly to those in need, we also give monthly to a ministry that is reaching Jewish people with the gospel.

The breakdown of our monthly distribution of undesignated funds is as follows:

1. From the giving portion—Mission of the Month (70 percent), Needy of the Month (15 percent), ministry to Jewish people (15 percent)
2. From the operating portion—bills, facilities maintenance, and pastor's compensation

This method permits distribution of God's money without needing a missions committee to decide who gets what, based on a best guess of how much money will come in for the year. It likewise dispenses with the need for a finance committee to set budget goals for the year. God has consistently outperformed any goals we might have set in both giving and operating budgets.

Paying the Pastor

Most pastors will undoubtedly not think highly of facilities maintenance and the pastor's compensation being at the tail end of the funds distribution. However, nothing we could have done would have backed up our commitment to missions more convincingly or rebuked the destructive materialism of our culture more persuasively. It has indeed worked wonderfully in breaking the mindset that we had to function as other churches do, where the two top priorities are to own or enlarge facilities and pay the pastor a competitive salary, with little left over for missions.

We have experienced some rather interesting unintended consequences, such as eliminating the excuse "We pay them enough, so let them do the work" and encouraging volunteerism in the congregation by discouraging any sense of entitlement in us as pastors. We stop and think, "If we can't teach effectively the biblical view of giving, why should we be paid more?"

We recently made a minor modification in funds distribution within the two categories to address the inconsistency of the monthly amount of pastor's compensation. This was done in response to the desire of the growing number of people who tithe to support more adequately vital ministry both inside and outside The Gathering. We will continue faithfully to adjust our corporate life to God's work among us and through us, in the location and circumstances he has given. Not every church will choose to collect and distribute their financial resources as we do. But our testimony is that God has blessed us mightily as we have remained faithful to what he is showing us.

Our resolve has been put to the test from time to time. For example, when we decided as a congregation to get a facility of our own instead of renting, we also drew a split of 65 percent to give away. A successful businessman and member of the Core Group said, "We can't do this. We're going to have to use some of the giving money to buy property." I (Rosie) replied, "You're right! We can't do it, but God can. We never touch his money. Let's see what he'll do." Within just four years (with no appeals) our fifteen-year mortgage had been paid off. God moves on the hearts of his people!

The Gathering is a healthy, growing church. It is a covenanting, praying, giving church. We live by what Jesus said: "If you

give, you will receive. Your gift will return to you in full measure, pressed down, shaken together to make room for more,
and running over. Whatever measure you use in giving—large
or small—it will be used to measure what is given back to you"
(Luke 6:38). God generously fills whatever size container we
present. We choose our own container. We can live with that.

Corporate Planning

Is the tendency in your church to plan next year's budget and
then pray for God to bless your plan? Would it be more faithful to pray first for what God has in mind and then adjust to
that, following God's direction as you proceed?

Henry Blackaby and Claude King aptly describe what God
wants to accomplish through your church:[9]

1. Realize that God does not just stand by waiting to bless
   our plan.
2. Recognize that God is more interested in working
   through us than in what we can do for him.
3. Understand that God wants us to follow him daily, not
   just to follow our plan.
4. Acknowledge that God is already at work around us
   and that he wants us to join in with that.
5. Clarify what God is telling us, without our own desires
   and agendas thrown in.
6. Let God work out the details of timing.
7. Wait on God until he tells us what to do next.

Corporate Lifestyle

Corporate planning is one of the major issues your church
must face in its desire to be a faithful, giving community. The
other major issue is corporate lifestyle.

The real "bottom line" is adjusting the corporate lifestyle to
what God is doing. The church that seeks God's kingdom in
the spiritual sense of worship and holiness but does not seek

God's kingdom by ordering its entire life accordingly is not a faithful church. A faithful church is marked by a generous lifestyle. It is a giving community guided in all of its decisions by God's direction regarding the distribution of resources dedicated to God's purposes.

The trouble, says Howard Snyder in *Liberating the Church,* is that "America's churches breathe the atmosphere of self-protection and self-aggrandizement. They run after the same things the world does. The church is not free for the Kingdom. Its sickness is symbolized by the average church budget: eighty or ninety percent spent on itself, a pittance for the rest of the world."[10]

Is your church like that? Is your church oriented mainly toward its own survival? If that is the case, your church is not a healthy church, and it likely will not thrive if it even survives.

Contrast the picture of "America's churches" with a different kind of church, one that resists the double unfaithfulness of survival orientation and materialism. This church is constantly looking for where God is at work so the people can join in with him. They also are in agreement with Ron Sider, as stated in *Rich Christians in an Age of Hunger,* "the Bible clearly and repeatedly teaches that God is at work in history exalting the poor and casting down the rich who got that way by oppressing or neglecting the poor. In that sense, God is on the side of the poor. He has a special concern for them because of their vulnerability."[11] Therefore, since God is at work throughout history helping the poor, and this church sees the application in their own community, they decide to adjust their corporate lifestyle accordingly. In doing so, they are in obedience to Scripture and are imitators of God. By tangibly, consistently sharing God's concern for the poor, they are becoming a giving community.

Following are ten guidelines that signify a biblically faithful, giving community:

1. Intentional community that nurtures an atmosphere of love and faithfulness among members
2. Servant leadership that builds up believers for the work of the ministry
3. Prayerful planning in order to join God's work, following God's direction
4. Equity budgeting that seeks a balance between missions and operations
5. Kingdom orientation, which leads to sharing programs, equipment, and staff resources with other churches, and which also leads to planting new churches rather than continually expanding facilities
6. Property use that prioritizes making facilities available to outside groups, utilizing land for community needs such as commuter parking, recreation, and garden plots
7. Wise energy use, avoiding waste in heating, cooling, and lighting in particular
8. Stewarding resources by recycling, repairing rather than replacing, minimizing consumption of water and paper products, and making use of the physical and human resources God has provided
9. Time management that respects discretionary time in planning and conducting meetings and that promotes gifts-based ministries
10. Prudent physical appearance—aesthetically pleasing and inviting, neither luxurious nor austere in architecture, furnishings, and landscaping

If the majority of church members have not resolved the issue of treasure in heaven versus storing up treasure on earth, their individual lifestyles inevitably will be reflected in the corporate lifestyle of the church. Conversely, the church's lifestyle has a powerful modeling effect on members' lifestyles. People notice what their church is doing and often take that as permission for their own actions. They may think, "My church wants the latest and the biggest and the best of everything, so why shouldn't I?" or "My church doesn't give to missions, really, so why should I?" and "The church doesn't recycle or conserve heat or electricity, so why should I?"

The church is a city on a hill, whose beacon of light illumines the darkness of the sinfulness in the surrounding society. It is also a bastion of hope for those who gather within, waging their own never-ending battle with the double unfaithfulness of survival orientation and materialism. If the people of God are to gain and preserve a giving spirit, then the church must be a giving community. When *both* the individual members' lifestyles *and* the church's corporate lifestyle are faithful and generous, a church has its greatest influence for Christ.

For Reflection and Discussion

1. What do you think the checkbook of your church would reveal about what it thinks of God? What does *your* personal checkbook reveal?
2. Before reading Deuteronomy 14:23 about the purpose of the tithe, what did you think was its purpose?
3. Since Scripture gives examples of the tithe before the Law was instituted (Abraham and Jacob), and since both Jesus and Paul went beyond the tithe and encouraged generous giving, what would you expect to see in a faithful small church?
4. "Live simply so that others may simply live" is not a one-time decision but a lifetime of choices. Which of the "affluenza" questions caused you to reexamine your lifestyle and choices?
5. Many pastors hesitate to speak about giving for fear that people will view them as self-serving, even though the Bible speaks more about money than either salvation or God's love. Who in your church *could* speak convincingly on this topic for the benefit of the church?

6. What is your church's attitude toward giving to the poor and to the Jewish people? What arguments can you find in Scripture for doing so?

7. Those who attend The Gathering Church cannot wait to see where they get to give their money each month, because they are part of the process. How are the people of your church involved in decisions regarding giving?

8. The text reveals how funds are received and counted in The Gathering. For disbursement, check-writing is done by the treasurer rather than the financial secretary. All checks are counter-signed. How is this biblical? How does it protect the individuals and the church? What changes, if any, does your church need to make in this area?

9. Which of the ten guidelines for a biblically faithful, giving community got your attention (p. 145)? How can your church improve in that area or those areas?

10. People have fewer discretionary hours than they did twenty years ago. Since giving includes time and talents as well as money, how has your church adjusted its schedule to allow people to give as generously as possible in all areas?

Getting Started

1. If you are considering implementing participatory worship services without regular sermons, you can ease the transition somewhat by offering a time-limited series of short sermons on your church becoming a biblically faithful, giving community. (This might be a good idea for any church, regardless of your plans for the future.)

2. If you have small groups in your church, encourage them to discuss the "affluenza" questions and to hold one another accountable in making changes in their lifestyles.

3. If you are intrigued by the experience of The Gathering Church budgeting "after the fact," put down on paper

how it might work for you. What categories and splits would you consider? What individuals and groups would you like to include in your corporate giving? What priority would you give to paying your pastor? to improving your facilities?

4. Ask your leadership group to review the ten guidelines for a biblically faithful, giving community and to seek prayerfully the Lord's leading with any concerns they might have.

1 1

living in the SPIRIT

---

ideas for IMPROVING your church's ministry

51. Four essential guidelines for a biblical view of dying to self
52. Four guideposts for confirming the Holy Spirit's leading into fruitfulness
53. Five biblical guidelines for evaluating the Spirit-life of your church

---

The key to a healthy church is giving oneself, individually and corporately, to the Lord. This is true for all ten biblically life-transforming activities that produce healthy churches:

1. **Shepherding** is giving oneself to the Good Shepherd for the privilege of tending the flock.
2. **Gathering** is giving oneself to meeting with God's people in God's presence for his purpose.
3. **Covenanting** is giving oneself to God's people in love and faithfulness.
4. **Ministering** is giving oneself to serving others in the name of Jesus.
5. **Studying** is giving oneself to knowing and having the mind of Christ.
6. **Worshiping** is giving oneself to the sacrifice of praise and humble adoration of an awesome God.
7. **Praying** is giving oneself to claiming victory in Jesus and enforcing the victory of light over darkness.

8. **Giving** is giving oneself to putting God first both in living and giving.
9. **Living** in the Spirit is giving oneself to dying to self-centeredness and living with Spirit-filled fruitfulness.
10. **Witnessing** is giving oneself to adding new believers and churches to the kingdom.

In this list, we see how important it is to die to a self-centered lifestyle in order to live a generous, Christ-centered lifestyle. That is living in the Spirit: dying to self-centeredness and living with Spirit-filled fruitfulness. The small church has the advantage in being a Spirit-formed church, abiding in the Holy Spirit for the releasing of his presence and power throughout the life of the church.

Dying to Self

We live in a world of overindulgence and inflated egos. We see it in our churches too. Rather than generous lifestyles, we often see addiction to the consumption of material things and compulsion toward personal power and prestige. Sadly, we also see the result: leanness of soul.

Putting God first in everything is an issue of the soul. Addictions and compulsions are putting *me* first, and that reduces one's soul. God forewarns us. When Israel rebelled in the wilderness, the people experienced what we likewise encounter when we rebel in our wilderness of learning to put God first: "They lusted excessively in the desert and tempted God in the wilderness, so He let them have what they wanted, but sent leanness within their soul" (Psalm 106:14-15, Berkeley).

Healthy Doctrine

Putting God first and dying to self-centeredness also is a doctrinal issue. When a doctrinal issue is at stake, tension arises between orthodoxy and orthopraxy, or right thinking versus right living. People sometimes tend to overemphasize sound doctrine while overlooking the healthfulness of doctrine. In *The Unnecessary Pastor,* Marva Dawn and Eugene Peterson refer to this as a tension between "sound" doctrine and "healthy" doctrine.[1] The two need not be in conflict. Right thinking leads to right living and, conversely, wrong thinking to wrong living. They go together.

Dawn and Peterson also differentiate "healthy" words from "diseased" words. "Words and living are the heads and tails of the same coin. When words are wrong—diseased— they cause illness; they infect the soul."[2] They are wrong not only doctrinally but also in their application. Yet even when the words are right—healthy words—we may incorrectly limit them to being doctrinally "sound" words as opposed to also being health-giving words.

Dawn and Peterson use Paul's letters to Timothy to note the importance of these distinctions:

> Sometimes "teaching" is translated as "doctrine" and so we get the impression that orthodoxy is at issue. But this isn't quite right. For Timothy is given a mandate to teach in a way that brings *health* to people. Words in Ephesus have gotten sick; the "godless chatter" in Ephesus is infecting the souls of people with disease. It is important not to see Timothy as a defender of orthodoxy, as someone who argues for the truth of the gospel. He is a teacher responsible for speaking in such a way that people get healthy again.[3]

We run into issues throughout the Bible that reflect the need to keep sound doctrine focused on health and to replace diseased words with healthy ones. We need to understand this, especially if we are to fully grasp the idea that a healthy church is healthy people. Getting it right will greatly help us not only in *defending* the truth but also in *living* the truth.

How are we to live out the biblical concept of dying to self? Unfortunately, we can easily miss the mark. One of the more troublesome errors is to "hate" one's self, where the focus is on introspection, boasting of one's weaknesses and crucifying one's self to refrain from sinning—or in the extreme version—to keep from losing one's salvation. Small churches need to be on guard to protect against creating a potentially cultlike environment with such fear-filled, diseased words. We need to heed Paul's warning in 2 Corinthians 11:4 about those who too easily submit to a different gospel.

Health-giving words in the four guidelines below are a biblical corrective to wrong words concerning dying to self.

1. On the matter of introspection for the purpose of hating or denying oneself, Gordon Fee writes in *Paul, the Spirit, and the People of God*:

    > Focused on the inner struggle, we can scarcely see Christ or walk confidently in the way of the Spirit. Instead of living out the fruit of the Spirit, in constant thankfulness for what the Spirit is doing in our lives and in the lives of others, our individualistic faith turns sourly narcissistic— aware of our personal failures before God, frustrated at our imperfections, feigning the love, joy, peace, and gentleness we wish were real. Our turmoil crowds out openness to the Spirit himself.[4]

2. Paul's main point regarding boasting is that we are to boast *in* our weakness rather than *of* our weakness (2 Corinthians 9-13).

3. We have already been crucified with Christ and no longer live, but Christ lives in us (Galatians 2:20). Therefore, crucifixion of self is not ongoing, but dying to self by dying to sin in this world occurs daily (John 12:25; cf. Romans 8:16-17).

4. Sin management is not a matter of salvation but of sanctification, that is, living a radically new life given by the Holy Spirit, convicting us to hate the way we are living

when we sin and empowering us to live righteously.

We must not teach a different gospel or allow narcissistic introspection to crowd out our openness to our radically new life in the Holy Spirit. Our focus needs to be on the Spirit, not on ourselves (Galatians 5:16-24). Romans 8:6-7 states:

> Obsession with self ... is a dead end; attention to God leads us out into the open, into a spacious, free life. Focusing on the self is the opposite of focusing on God. Anyone completely absorbed in self ignores God, ends up thinking more about self than God. That person ignores who God is and what he is doing *(The Message)*.

When we are obsessed with thoughts about our lives in the world, we are living in the flesh. That is a dead end! The heart of the gospel is *resurrection* (1 Corinthians 15). The gospel is not dead in the body but alive in the Spirit. The Lord has "set before you life and death, the blessing and the curse: Therefore choose life" (Deuteronomy 30:19, Berkeley). Set your mind on the things of the Spirit. Live in the Spirit. Choose life and be blessed.

Living in the Spirit

People in healthy churches freely and naturally praise God for who he is and are thankful for God's works. They do so boasting in their own weakness and boasting in God's glory revealed in doing the things that delight the Lord.[5] They are living in the Spirit.

Spirit-Formed Life

In *Living the Spirit-Formed Life,* Jack Hayford makes a helpful distinction between the Spirit-filled and Spirit-formed life, and presents steps toward a Spirit-formed life, as set forth in Scripture:

1. Be *Spirit-born* by repenting for your sins and by putting your faith in Jesus Christ as your *Savior*, verifying the

commitment by obeying Jesus Christ as *Lord* and being baptized in water (see Acts 2:38, 39).

2. Be *Spirit-filled* by receiving the promise Jesus gave that his followers shall receive power—power to move in new dimensions of worship, praise, prayer, service, and witness (see Acts 1:5-8; 2:1-4).

3. Be *Spirit-formed* by recognizing that the entry door of new birth and the birthright blessing of Holy Spirit fullness are only *beginnings*—both calling us as believers to *growth* in Christ's likeness and *discipleship* under His lordship (see Romans 12:1,2; Acts 2:42,46,47).[6]

Step number three entails abiding in Holy Spirit fullness for God's presence and power to be released in and through our lives. Hayford likens this to "rivers of living water," referring to Jesus' call to his followers: "He who believes in Me, as the Scripture has said, out of his heart will flow rivers of living water" (John 7:38, NKJV). Hayford suggests that some of these rivers are:

- Rivers of gifts of the Spirit
- Rivers of ministry
- Rivers of worship
- Rivers of prayer
- Rivers of witness
- Rivers of revelation
- Rivers of peace
- Rivers of fruit of the Spirit[7]

Fruit of the Spirit

The fruit of the Spirit is direct evidence that we are abiding in the Holy Spirit. Fullness in God's Spirit equals fruitfulness. In *The Wonderful Spirit-Filled Life*, Charles Stanley expands on Galatians 5:22-23 to help us recognize the evidences of fruitful living in the Spirit, as follows:

When we abide in Him and allow Him to live His life

through us, the result is character that endures the chaos of life. The fruit of the Spirit is—

- Love for those who do not love in return
- Joy in the midst of painful circumstances
- Peace when something you were counting on doesn't come through
- Patience when things aren't going fast enough for you
- Kindness toward those who treat you unkindly
- Goodness toward those who have been intentionally insensitive to you
- Faithfulness when friends have proved unfaithful
- Gentleness toward those who have handled you roughly
- Self-control in the midst of intense temptation[8]

Spiritual Markers

Stanley further gives four "spiritual markers," or guideposts, for indicating and confirming that the Holy Spirit is leading us into fruitfulness. These help us answer the question, "How do we know we want and are doing what God wants?"

The first marker is *peace*. As a fruit of the Spirit, peace, or lack of it, is often a first indication of the Spirit's intention for us. When we are inwardly unsettled, God still may be saying that we want and are doing what God wants. On the other hand, when we are unsettled or have a "check" in our spirit (a conviction that something is not right), God may be saying we are not being led into fruitfulness. Paul says that the peace of God operates like a guard to protect our hearts and minds, even when we do not fully comprehend our circumstances (Philippians 4:7). God provides a guard, but not a guarantee. To discern what inner peace or a sense of foreboding or hesitancy is about, we should look to other markers as well.

The *conscience* is a second marker. According to Stanley, the Holy Spirit uses the conscience as an instant warning device, evaluator and discerner, and judge and jury. When good things are not God's best for us, how do we know? How do we learn about the presence or absence of sin? "The conscience is one of the Holy Spirit's primary tools through which He communicates with believers. Don't ignore the warnings and promptings of the conscience. To do so is to run the risk of missing God."[9]

A third marker is the *Word of God*. Says Stanley, "If you want to know what the Holy Spirit thinks about something, read the Bible."[10] Also, "The Holy Spirit will never lead you where the Word of God forbids you to go."[11] And finally, "Peace or no peace. Guilty conscience or no guilty conscience. The Word of God stands. It is the final authority for the Spirit-filled believer. The Spirit-filled life is a life lived in accordance with the teachings of the Scripture—whether one feels like it or not and whether it bears witness with one's spirit or not."[12]

Wisdom is a fourth marker. The Holy Spirit uses wisdom to personalize biblical principles and advice from others. On one hand, the Bible might not prohibit something, but that very thing might be wrong for me at this time. On the other hand, the Bible may permit something that is not good for me at this time. Paul therefore says, "Everything is permissible for me—allowable and lawful; but not all things are helpful—good for me to do, expedient and profitable when considered with other things" (1 Corinthians 6:12, Amplified). Something that is right for you may not be right for me. "The Holy Spirit guides the believer in the way of wisdom. To refuse to live wisely is to ignore the leading of the Holy Spirit."[13]

Spirit-Formed Church

Living in the Spirit means we follow the leading of the Holy Spirit in every part of our lives (Galatians 5:25). This applies equally to individual believers and to the corporate body of believers. Jesus calls us to Holy Spirit fullness and fruitfulness.

Our individual Spirit-formed lives are integrated into Spirit-formed churches.

Greg Ogden has a diagram in his book *The New Reformation* of the main ingredients of Spirit formation. His illustration shows how the Holy Spirit connects and unifies the Bible, body, and believer (see below).[14]

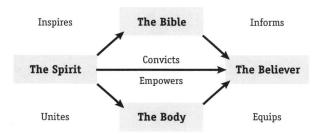

The Spirit inspires translations of the Bible and through them informs (and *inwardly forms*) the believer. The Spirit also unites the body of believers and equips the believer through that body. Moreoever, as just noted, the Spirit directly convicts and empowers the believer to live in the Spirit.

Several views in Scripture shape a vision of the church as a corporate entity living in the Spirit, as a Spirit-formed body. In addition, Revelation 3:1 provides an example of what a Spirit-formed church does *not* look like. The church in Sardis thought it was doing very well. It had a reputation of being "alive," but the Lord said, "You are dead." The Sardis believers were full of religious deeds and were outwardly very busy. Yet they did not know the reality of living in the Spirit. They needed to wake up!

In contrast with the church in Sardis, Hayford summarizes five other biblical views of the church that serve as guidelines for evaluating the Spirit-life of your church:[15]

1. Loving family (1 John; 2 John; 3 John). Is your church a united and anointed fellowship, pursuing purity and over-

coming the world, the flesh, and the devil?

2. Ministry force (Ephesians). Is your church a body (army) moving against the forces of evil?

3. Obedient people (James). Are the people in your church being called to integrity, to their responsibilities for one another, and to accountability for responsible action in response to their reading of Scripture?

4. Worshiping host (1 Peter). Is your church a holy priest-hood of believers?

5. Spirit-filled community (Acts). Is your church a spiritu-ally gifted and caring assembly, abiding in prayer and unimpressed by either their opponents' or their own achievements?

The church is a charismatic community. Howard Snyder makes this point in his book, *The Problem of Wineskins*:

According to the New Testament, the church is a charis-matic organism, not an institutional organization. The church is the result of the grace (Greek, *charis*) of God. It is through grace that the church is saved (Eph. 2:8) and through the exercise of spiritual gifts of grace *(charismata)* that the church is edified (Rom. 12:6-8; Eph. 4:7-16; 1 Pet. 4:10-11). Thus the church is, by definition, *charismatic*.[16]

Would you characterize your church as a living organism, or is it simply a religious organization? In the Bible metaphors for the church, such as body, bride, family and flock, embody life. Does your church embody life, or is it encased in organi-zational structures that stifle the presence and power of the Holy Spirit throughout every area of church life? Is your church alive, or is it dead?

The healthy church chooses the charismatic model rather than the institutional model. The healthy church in biblical terms is the Spirit-formed church, where "the whole body is fitted together perfectly. As each part does its own special work, it helps the other parts grow, so that the whole body is

healthy and growing and full of love" (Ephesians 4:16).
Therefore, choose life.

For Reflection and Discussion

1. This would be a good time to review what a healthy church looks like. As you consider healthy areas in your church, which area(s) do you also note that could use some attention?

2. If believers refer to themselves as "sinners" versus "saints who sin," they will hold a less than positive mindset. Eugene Peterson stresses the importance of choosing right words. Give another example of word choice that could affect outcome in your church.

3. Jesus died for the whole of people's lives. How have you observed that disparaging or "hating" one's self keeps you or others from living out that truth?

4. Whether individually or corporately, introspection can take on a life of its own. What are the hazards Gordon Fee warns against (p. 152)? Has your church experienced any of these?

5. How do Jack Hayford's ideas about living in the Spirit clarify your thinking (p. 153–154)?

6. What was your response to Hayford's list of "rivers of living water" (p. 154)?

7. Christians often list the fruit of the Spirit without specifically knowing how to identify their own fruitfulness. How did Charles Stanley's list make this clearer for you (p. 155)?

8. People frequently use one "spiritual marker" when making decisions, but Stanley says four are needed (p. 155–156). Which one(s) do you need to be more intentional about?

9. Evaluate your church as a Spirit-formed church. Which of the five biblical guidelines do you need to work on (p. 157–158)?

10. How did you respond to the question at the end of the chapter, "Is your church alive, or is it dead?" On what do you base your answer?

Getting Started

1. To help guard against a cultlike view of dying to self, hold your church up to the mirror of the four biblical guidelines on pages 152–153. What do you see?
2. Again, if you have small groups or desire a good topic for discussion in another venue, consider Charles Stanley's list of nine evidences of fruitful living in the Spirit (p. 155). Suggest that participants pray for and spur one another on to good works and changed lives.
3. Apply Stanley's concept of spiritual markers (peace, conscience, Word of God, and wisdom) to the corporate body. On what occasions have those confirmed that the Holy Spirit was leading you into fruitfulness? On what occasions *should* they have been heeded but were not?
4. Ask your leadership group to review the five guidelines for evaluating the Spirit-life of your church (p. 157–158) and to prayerfully seek the Lord's leading with any concerns they might have.

1 2

witnessing

---

ideas for IMPROVING your church's ministry

54. Recommendations concerning healthy evangelism
55. A recommendation of a lesser known but great motivator for evangelism
56. Three important questions for assessing the effectiveness of traditional altar call–oriented worship services
57. Three important questions for assessing the effectiveness of modern seeker-oriented worship services
58. Ten pointers for developing the relationship evangelism skills of every member of the congregation
59. Three methods of corporate evangelism
60. Nine ways to birth new churches

God has a grand design for faithful, healthy, great small churches. He watches over the sheep, gathering and nourishing them with covenantal love. The flock is renewed every day, as God equips them for ministry, calls them to responsible action, and inhabits their praises. He is answering their prayers as they give to God first and as they live in the Spirit and tell others about Jesus. God's design for the church is that we gather and go.

The first nine life-transforming activities of healthy churches encompass the gathering aspect of God's design. This last one, witnessing, is about going. Jesus told us to go into the world, to tell other people about him, and to make them disciples. In other words, healthy churches abide in the first nine areas concurrently with determined activity in the tenth. The option is not to gather *or* go. It is not to gather *then* go. Rather, it is gather *and* go.

Witnessing is discussed here in terms of adding new believers and churches to the kingdom while acting with urgency and abiding in discipleship. This is another area of life-transforming activity where the small church has the advantage: in evangelistic effectiveness and innovative multiplication.

Birthing Believers in Christ

Too many churches today just sit and wait for people to come to them. However, having great programs, pastors, and facilities is not what Jesus is talking about. Churches urgently need to do just what Jesus says: Go into the world, tell people the good news, and make disciples of them. Tom Clegg and Warren Bird in their book *Lost in America* offer reasons for going:

1. If people who are unchurched in America comprised a nation, it would be the fifth largest nation in the world.
2. "Virtually half the churches across the United States did not record the conversion of one person last year."[1]
3. "In the past fifty years, U.S. churches have failed to gain an additional 2 percent of the American population."[2]
4. "'Nine out of ten pastors call their church *evangelistic*. However, less than one out of three church attenders has shared his or her faith in Christ with a non-Christian within the past twelve months.' Something is desperately wrong with this picture!"[3]

Healthy Evangelism

Indeed, something is desperately wrong with the picture of the evangelism enterprise of our churches. Though this is an extremely important matter, we just as strongly acknowledge that, while evangelism is a top priority, it is not *the* purpose of the church.

In a healthy church, witnessing springs naturally from the dynamic of the vital worship and vibrant discipleship of the loving, serving community of believers. Witnessing neither stands alone, nor is it a program strategy to sustain church membership, a strategy "to invite people in, with the winking assurance that 'everything' can remain the same," writes Walter Brueggemann in *Biblical Perspectives on Evangelism*.[4] Evangelism in a healthy church is not used to pad the pews.

This "winking assurance" that nothing changes when people identify with a local church brings to light the fact that converts too often are brought into churches without realizing that being part of the body of Christ means being a citizen in the kingdom of Christ. They have heard the good news, but have heard nothing about the kingdom. Healthy churches proclaim the good news *and* the kingdom life. The common propensity of unhealthy churches, however, is to collapse evangelism into the act of only proclaiming the good news.

Brueggemann points out that kingdom proclamation is far more than that. It includes (1) proclaiming the good news of victory over death in all of its forms and deliverance from all forms of individual and institutional bondage and (2) appropriating the good news of the transformation of individual lives and the life of the community of believers.[5] Kingdom proclamation cannot be reduced to simple formulas and slogans. Neither is it mere tricks for growth of the local church. It is truth for new converts to be transformed. Howard Snyder observes in *Liberating the Church* that televangelism disembodies the gospel by separating it from the witness of a local body of believers, and even disembodies Christ by enlisting people to join the head without being joined to the body, the local church.[6]

Kingdom proclamation conveys the undiluted, uncompromising message that conversion to Jesus Christ means active participation in the body of Christ and willing commitment to the kingdom of God. Proclamation of the good news and its appropriation are part and parcel. Conversion is germinal, not terminal!

Urgent Evangelism

Evangelism ultimately operates within the context of our understandings of the establishment of God's kingdom and the return of Jesus. Christians hold a wide range of understandings of these issues. A variety of theologies appropriate apocalyptic biblical literature in light of the "glorious appearing of Jesus" (Titus 2:13), yet to come. Those who take this approach differ significantly on details. We recommend a lesser known, but highly motivating view that does not share the escapist and fatalistic overtones of some other views within this approach. This perspective asserts that before the return of Christ, there will be widespread persecution of Christ's followers and "unless that time of calamity is shortened, the entire human race will be destroyed. But it will be shortened for the sake of God's chosen ones" (Matthew 24:22). Therefore, we must do all we can now in witnessing to Christ's redeeming love so that there will be fewer people at that time who have not heard and hence the days of persecution might be cut short.[7]

Other approaches accept the imagery and details of apocalyptic literature as speaking exclusively to the age in which it was written, rather than as a description of a future time. Nonetheless, all of the perspectives hold some understanding of God's kingdom as a present, but not fully complete reality and have some view of Jesus' ongoing and yet-to-be-fully-realized presence in the Church and in the world. All approaches share two characteristics: a belief in a kingdom begun in Jesus, but to be completed; and a belief in the agency of God *and* human beings in the completion of the kingdom. These beliefs—in the coming fulfillment of the kingdom and in the agency of human beings in active witness in fulfilling the kingdom—demand a sense of urgency for evangelism.

All Christians who believe that our Lord is not willing that any should perish and all who believe that we are chosen instruments in the process of helping others reconcile with God should feel an urgency to be faithful witnesses in the present day. If we accept that we are not only participants in God's grace and citizens of God's kingdom, but also agents of that grace and kingdom, we cannot deny the pressing nature of our task to bear witness to Christ. When we further realize that both the redemption of people and the well-being of the Church are at stake, and that our actions *now* might shorten the persecution of believers later, then we have powerful motivation indeed to make evangelism a part of how we live.

Relationship Evangelism

As important as a vital sense of urgency is for saving the lost, such a sense does not in and of itself accomplish much. Urgency to seek and save the lost must be nurtured in the environment of a healthy church. Evangelism will not make an unhealthy church healthy, but a healthy church will make evangelism effective. Only a healthy church can prepare itself for witnessing during tribulation as well as during normal times of comfort and celebration.

Effective evangelism is the fruit of a covenanting body of believers who are faithful to Jesus' instruction in John 13:34-35: "I am giving you a new commandment: Love each other. Just as I have loved you, you should love each other. Your love for one another will prove to the world that you are my disciples." Our love for one another identifies us as Jesus' disciples and therefore lends credibility to our witness. When unbelievers see that we love one another, they see that our relationship with Jesus is real. That is good news for small churches, because loving one another is the natural domain of the healthy small church.

Our relationships with one another are tied directly to our relationship with Jesus, and in evangelism they are tied directly to unbelievers. In relationship with us, the unbeliever sees who we are as disciples of Jesus and hears what we have to say about Jesus. Abiding in discipleship in a covenanting community of believers is therefore the basic context for relationship evangelism.

Small churches must be careful not to give up their advantage in evangelistic effectiveness. Some have sacrificed their relational evangelistic context by holding on to the traditional altar call–oriented worship service as their primary form of evangelism. If you are in such a church, you might ask yourself a few questions: Are you impeding the natural flow of evangelistic outreach as a byproduct of God-centered worship? Does the emotional build-up to the altar call suggest to people that this is the church's official invitation to sinners and that church members merely need to get them to church to hear it? Is your worship experience being diverted from practicing the presence of the Lord to anticipating the salvation of sinners? Perhaps both evangelism and worship are getting the proverbial short end of the stick.

Other small churches have bought into the modern seeker-oriented worship service. Yet again, questions arise: Is your desire for cultural relevance crowding out your passion for truth? Has evangelism at your church been reduced to a "feverishness" about your attempts to continuously meet the needs of the community and make it easier for your neighbors to identify with what you are doing? Has evangelism been subordinated to entertainment? Marva Dawn gives a strong warning in *Reaching Out without Dumbing Down:*

> If people are saved by a spectacular Christ, will they find
> him in the fumbling of their own devotional life or in the

humble services of local parishes where pastors and organists make mistakes? Will a glitzy portrayal of Christ nurture in new believers his character of willing suffering and sacrificial obedience? Will it create an awareness of the idolatries of our age and lead to repentance?[8]

Perhaps your church should be less feverish in bringing the world into the church and more intentional in bringing the church to the world. Ask yourself two other questions: How is your church visible to the surrounding community? Do they see a building at a certain location or do they see people who are involved in their daily lives—at work, at school, at the store, on the street, in the restaurant?

We have found with our four-legged sheep that the work of reproducing sheep belongs to the members of the flock. In a healthy flock the *sheep* are birthing lambs; we should do as little as possible to help. In other words, the work of evangelism belongs to the members of the body of Christ, and when someone is bearing fruit in ministry, let him or her run with it. Thus, when someone has a friend who expresses interest in the Lord, let that person not say, "You need to talk to my pastor." Encourage him or her to lead the person to the Lord. It is good to remember that sheep produce sheep, and when they are actually lambing, the shepherd should do as little as possible.

Clegg and Bird in *Lost in America* list ten pointers on how to create caring personal relationships for effective relationship evangelism:

1. Start where you are, with family and friends whom you already know.
2. Be yourself with them.
3. Include them in *your* interests and hobbies, building and deepening your relationships in the process.
4. Do other things together, cultivating intentional friendships.
5. Pray for them regularly by name and recognize their needs.
6. Find ways genuinely to serve them.

7. Be especially prayerful and available when they are facing tough times.
8. Respond with "I care" statements and make sure your actions speak louder than your words.
9. Ask leading questions rather than telling them answers.
10. Invite them to take a step toward God; ask them what God is teaching them; and ask them how they would like you to pray for them.[9]

The hardest part of all this for most people is *starting* spiritual conversations. In their book and the accompanying course titled *Becoming a Contagious Christian*, Bill Hybels and Mark Mittelberg offer excellent advice for starting spiritual conversations in a natural way, in a style that fits you. They cover six different personal styles of relationship evangelism: confrontational, intellectual, testimonial, interpersonal, invitational, and service.[10] The Gathering Church includes this course as one of the core courses required for membership (see Chapter 7).

Corporate Evangelism

Spiritual conversations can take place just about anywhere, but at The Gathering, we provide two forums for them: small groups and a monthly fellowship brunch. These are two of our three primary corporate methods of evangelism. (The third, church planting, we discuss in the next section.)

We make use of small groups for "side-door" evangelism. Carl George observes in his book on small group leadership that small groups are becoming the most effective entry point to churches worldwide.[11]

Small groups come in a variety of types, including special interest, support, study, and service. At The Gathering, we presently have a marriage group, parenting group, youth group, care groups, and men's and women's Bible study groups. Whatever the type, group members are all in contact with people who may be interested in joining a group such as theirs. As pre-Christian acquaintances, friends, or relatives (even those who may be intimidated or turned off by "church") begin to experience the atmosphere of acceptance, fellowship, and informal interaction, they begin to see the group as a safe place to ask questions and share thoughts. Spiritual conversations naturally occur.

The monthly fellowship brunch at The Gathering is held every second Sunday morning. We cancel our entire Sunday morning schedule to gather and eat together, enjoy one another's company, and engage in a common activity. We have a fivefold purpose:

1. To promote the priority of fellowship while respecting people's limited discretionary time during the week
2. To provide a safe and nonthreatening larger context for relationship evangelism, where guests perhaps already know some of the people and experience the fellowship of believers firsthand
3. To present ministry reports, opportunities, and issues (for example, visiting missionaries, Pregnancy Resource Service, Habitat for Humanity, Union Gospel Mission, TransWorld Radio, a video on persecuted Christians, and so on), with adequate time for full coverage and in-depth discussion
4. To produce something together as a congregation, such as packing hygiene kits for World Concern, packaging and labeling Bibles for Bibles for the World, or presenting a Christmas skit
5. To permit scheduled breaks for both students and teachers from Sunday school assignments and preparations

We take special delight in devoting the August brunch each year to baptism. We meet at a nearby county park for a picnic, singing, testimonies of those who are to be baptized, and a message on the meaning of baptism. Then the person who was most influential in leading each person to the Lord baptizes him or her in the adjoining lake.

Results

Christian Schwarz conducted a massive study in thirty-two countries on five continents and found that the evangelistic effectiveness of small churches far exceeds that of large churches:

> While the smallest churches (with an average attendance of 51) typically won 32 new people [to Christ] in the last five years, the megachurches (with an average attendance of 2,856) won 112 new persons [to Christ] during the same time period.... If we remember, though, that the megachurches are 56 times the size of the "minichurches," then the following calculation expresses the potential of the two categories far more realistically. If instead of a single church with 2,856 in worship we had 56 churches, each with 51 worshippers, these churches would, statistically, win 1,792 new people [to Christ] within five years—16 times the number the megachurch would win. Thus we can conclude that the evangelistic effectiveness of minichurches is statistically 1,600 percent greater than that of megachurches![12]

Since these figures are averages, notable exceptions are present at both ends of the size continuum. Nevertheless, Schwarz emphasizes that megachurches are not appropriate models for others. It would "be far more helpful to carefully examine the countless smaller churches manifesting high quality, strong growth, and innovative multiplication. If we need models at all, we should look for them in this category," says Schwarz.[13] We heartily agree. It is so good to be a small church!

Birthing Bodies of Christ

Schwarz's findings make a strong case for church multiplication, with existing churches being the major players. In fact, the most potent kingdom proclamation an existing church can make is planting another church.

Our third primary corporate method of evangelism is

church planting. Healthy churches are reproducing churches. We also want to remain true to our roots. We were planted and we will plant. We have an obligation to the kingdom to plant churches. In *Planting Growing Churches for the 21st Century,* Aubrey Malphurs writes:

> The idea is that planted churches reproduce themselves and make disciples by planting other churches. This is a process that will continue until the Savior returns. In fact, this is the true meaning of the Great Commission. If we desire to know how the early church understood Christ's commission, we can find the answer in the Book of Acts. Acts is a church-planting book because much of what takes place does so in the context of starting new churches. Therefore, it shouldn't surprise us when someone such as Peter Wagner says, *"The single most effective evangelistic methodology under heaven is planting new churches."*[14]

We read in Acts 2–14, about local churches being birthed in Jerusalem, Phoenicia, Cyprus, Antioch, Iconium, Lystra, and Derbe, and in chapters 15–20, we read about churches planted in Phillipi, Thessalonica, Berea, Athens, Corinth, and Ephesus. Speaking at the seminar "Bootcamp for Reproducing Churches," Michael Noel made these observations regarding the church plant in Antioch:[15]

1. "The power of the Lord was upon them," and many turned to the Lord (11:21).
2. The mother church supervised and nurtured the daughter church (11:22-24).
3. The mother church provided staff for the daughter church (11:25-27).
4. The believers in the daughter church demonstrated remarkable generosity and compassion (11:28-30).
5. Healthy churches prioritize kingdom expansion, in this case sending out gifted leadership in pursuit of the mission (13:2-3).

6. The leadership understood that the Holy Spirit was the prime mover—they were not franchising their own name (13:4).
7. Spiritual warfare confronted them wherever the kingdom reached into darkness (13:6-12).
8. The objective of evangelizing was in every case to leave a functioning church behind (14:21-22).
9. They appointed and multiplied leaders as soon as possible (14:23).
10. The church planters reported back to the mother church that a new church had been birthed (14:24-28).

Problems

If planting churches, as seen in the examples in Acts, "is the true meaning of the Great Commission," and if it is also true that "the single most effective evangelistic methodology is planting churches," then why have so few churches caught the vision?

One problem involves the status quo. A good many churches like things to stay the way they are. The facilities are serviceable, membership is stable, leadership is satisfactory, and finances are sufficient. They are stagnant churches, accepting their lot of growing older and witnessing less. As with increasing size, witnessing declines with age. The following statistics are revealing:[16]

- A church less than three years old requires three Christians to lead one person to Christ.
- A church between four and seven years old requires seven Christians to lead one person to Christ.
- A church more than ten years old requires eighty-five Christians to lead one person to Christ.

The conversion ratios are 3:1, 7:1, and 85:1. That's astounding! Another problem is related to strategy. Some churches are *not* satisfied with the status quo and believe their best strategy is through revitalization. However, according to Malphurs in *Vision America,* "the hard truth is that revitalizing ... churches involves much energy and large infusions of change, and many established churches will find that they are tired and that it is too painful to make the kinds of changes necessary for revival."

The problem is one of "old wineskins." While revitalization can be a viable strategy, we must remember that old wineskins do not stretch very well. Better to pour new wine into new wineskins than to risk bursting an old wineskin. Or, as is often said, "It's easier to birth a baby than to raise the dead!"

A third problem is having a survival mentality. Many small churches fear they could not survive the financial demands to plant a church, that only large churches have enough resources. However, participation in planting a new church can take many forms. Moreover, money follows mission. People give to a captivating mission that produces kingdom-building outcomes.

Options

Putting all problems aside, what are a small church's options for birthing new churches? Here are some ways Michael Noel proposed in his seminar for a small church to participate, either alone or in cooperation with others:[18]

1. Pioneering: commissioning a church planting team from the parent church to start a new congregation of either a similar or different style; this is referred to as a "parachute drop" and has the highest risk and stress
2. Branching: "hiving" or splitting off a core group from the parent church
3. Cell-based "daughtering": growing small groups to serve as the foundation for a new church plant
4. Unplanned parenting: splitting into two groups and growing into two separate churches; this is like an emergency Cesarean, when a church is unknowingly pregnant with a

large faction that is fighting for change and the mother's life is threatened unless the groups separate

5. Restarting: rebirthing at the same site when a declining or dysfunctional church changes leadership
6. Partnering: cooperating with one or more congregations to start a new church
7. Supporting: providing prayer, finances, and other resources to support a church plant, with primary leadership and direction coming from another source, such as a denomination or church planting organization (something like a baby shower)
8. Cross-cultural planting: hosting or sponsoring an ethnic congregation in your community.
9. Dying with dignity: closing a declining church and releasing the assets for new church development.

Your small church has choices for planting new churches, but none will be chosen without a vision. You must see yourself as a reproducing church and be intentional about taking the necessary steps to plant your first church using the method the Lord provides for you. One helpful step we have taken at The Gathering is making a commitment, as we continue to grow, to remain a small church of approximately 90 to 100 people regularly attending. That is a strong motivator to progress actively toward planting another church. This is a wonderful way for us to die to corporate self and serve our living Lord.

We are not alone in self-imposed restraint on building our own little kingdom. *Vital Ministry* magazine gives the example of Orlando (Florida) Community Church, which has an official policy of limiting growth to a predetermined number and then dividing to plant a new church. They have accomplished one successful church plant to date, Vista Community Church, on Orlando's south side. This is integral to OCC's commitment to stay "small, simple, and entirely straightforward."[19]

We too desire to be small, simple, and straightforward as we press forward in kingdom work as a reproducing church. God is awesome and is doing great things through our little church. More than us doing great things *for* God, we are thankful that God is doing great things *through* us (Psalm 115:1). In Christ, small truly is beautiful.

For Reflection and Discussion

1. Witnessing is frequently assigned to the preacher or the special few who really want to do it. What word or emotion *immediately* comes to mind when you hear the word *witnessing?*
2. The actual meaning of Jesus commissioning his disciples is, "As you are going ... make disciples." As one who desires to be obedient, list the places you go frequently. What people, by name if possible, do you know in each of those places who seem not yet to know Jesus?
3. Which people that you listed in question number two are you willing to put on a three-by-five index card and Pray Until Something Happens (PUSH)?
4. How reassuring is it to you to know that at least six styles of witnessing are effective? Why do you think The Gathering Church has included "Becoming a Contagious Christian" as a course to take before becoming a member?
5. What problems, if any, do you see with traditional altar call–oriented and modern seeker-oriented worship services?
6. What would you say are some of the strengths of the two forums (small groups and a monthly fellowship brunch) presented for facilitating spiritual conversations?
7. New Christians often have several pre-Christians as friends, so a good strategy is to have a mature Christian help evangelize those friends. How does your church reach out to the enthusiastic new Christian's contacts?

8. Too often new Christians are consigned to sitting in the pew until they can "grow up." Or else, they are treated as lone rangers and not even introduced to the body at all. Equally bad, they may be put to work in every conceivable way, such as teaching Sunday school, singing in the choir, taking nursery duty, or doing anything else others are tired of doing, even though they are baby Christians who need to be discipled. How has your church worked with new believers so their "conversion is germinal, not terminal"?

9. This chapter emphasized how one's view of the timing of Christ's return can influence the urgency one feels about witnessing. First, identify the view you hold. Second, explain how you have thought about witnessing in the context of that view.

10. When we are actively involved in seeing people come to Jesus as Lord and Savior, we are being obedient. Seeing the church multiply by planting churches where people live is equally important. A church's involvement in birthing new churches can take many forms. Which ideas from the list of nine choices on pages 173–174 do you think might be of interest to your church?

Getting Started

1. If your church has either altar call–oriented or seeker-oriented worship services, evaluate them using the questions on pages 166–167. What corrections, if any, need to be made?

2. Add Clegg and Bird's ten pointers for developing relationship evangelism skills (p. 167–168) to the curriculum at both the youth and adult levels in your teaching program.

3. Ask your leadership group to evaluate your church's vision for church multiplication. Is there a problem with the status quo? strategy? survival mentality? (See p. 172–173.)

4. Urge your leadership group to investigate the feasibility of each of the nine suggestions for planting new churches (p. 173–174). Consider whether the church would back their conclusions and suggestions.

epilogue

We've come a long way together through numerous issues and ideas. We have sought passionately to understand what God wants the local church to be. Perhaps you have come to a better realization of what your own church should be but are finding it difficult to imagine where to begin.

You are not alone. At The Gathering Church we are continuously refining our understanding of God's design for the local church while at the same time trying to adjust to God's specific desire for our church. We hope that the questions for reflection and discussion and the suggestions for getting started on improving your church's ministry will help you as you attempt to discover where God would have you go from here.

We understand that reflection and discussion do not automatically lead to *implementation*. We would encourage you to ask, Where is God already at work? What is already in our hand? You know you cannot be all things to all people, but as you were reading through the book, where did your spirit connect with "Yes, that's us" or "Now we know what that is and have a name for it"? Ask yourself how you could expand or improve in that area.

Implementation is a corporate as well as individual affair. It is beyond the scope of this book to provide all the details for corporate change. However, we do want to encourage you to involve other members of the congregation as soon as possible. If you are active in a particular ministry or serve on a board or committee in the church, you have a ready-made point of contact and forum for discussion. If you are the pastor, you will need to work with the congregation to recognize where God has already put human, physical, and spiritual resources into your corporate hand. Then as changes are made, you will want to find ways to celebrate the blessings. Let everyone in the congregation know that God is indeed at work in some very special areas of your church life.

We suggest an unlikely forum for your celebration: the annual meeting. We know that annual meetings have a reputation for being less than pleasurable experiences and poorly attended. It doesn't have to be that way. At The Gathering we make our annual meeting special by holding it on the first fellowship brunch Sunday of the year. We make it a point to celebrate anything in the past year that God has used to bless us and others through us. For example:

- We read the names of all the people who taught a class (nursery and upward)—we have them stand and applaud them and their efforts.
- We read the names of the people who tended the nursery, scheduled nursery workers, prepared the Communion elements, maintained the facility and grounds, coordinated the library, and others whose ministry usually does not receive recognition. We have them stand and receive applause.
- We acknowledge our various small-group ministries.
- We report the number of decisions made for Christ during the past year.
- We name those who were baptized and the children who were dedicated.
- We report how the financial giving of the congregation has blessed various people and organizations throughout the year—we highlight the total amount of our giving for the year and the responses of some of the recipients.
- We celebrate one or two areas where God has blessed our socks off.

Reading ministry reports is boring. We recommend that you distribute them for people to read before the meeting. The budget report can be even worse, causing rancor among people vying for control over some aspect of church life. By having a financial report for the previous year rather than a budget for the coming year, we can more easily focus on celebrating what God has done and on looking forward to what God *will* do through his people in the coming year. We expect to see how God is using us for his glory, and we enjoy watching him do it. Thus, our annual meeting is a high point of the year!

Does your church expect God to use you regularly for his glory? Do you enjoy watching God do that? To put it in another way, do you desire to be a *great* church? If so, this is our final recommendation: glorify God and enjoy him forever!

essential qualities of a
HEALTHY church[1]

Empowering Leadership

Pastors equip people to be used as God wants them to be used. The pastor invests the majority of his or her time discipling and equipping people to do the work of the ministry.

Key question: Does the leadership at our church motivate and equip people for ministry?

Reference: Ephesians 4:11-13

Loving Relationships

People share one another's burdens and celebrate one another's joys. There is a lot of laughter in our church. People share their time and resources with others both inside and outside the church body.

Key question: Is our church a place where people enjoy being together and truly care about one another's needs?

References: John 13:34-35; Acts 2:42-47; 1 Corinthians 12:26

Gift-Oriented Ministry[2]

Personal ministry involvement is matched with giftedness. People receive training, either within or outside our church for their ministries.

Key question: Are the ministries at our church consistent with the spiritual gifts of the people in the congregation?

References: Romans 12:6-8; 1 Corinthians 12:11; Ephesians 4:11-16; 1 Peter 4:10-11

Disciple-making Small Groups[3]

Small groups are available for any combination of understanding and applying Scripture, participating with others in prayer, experiencing loving relationships, and pursuing mutual interests.

Key question: Are small, intentional gatherings at our church available to everyone, and do they meet people's needs to become more like Christ?

References: Ephesians 4:15; Hebrews 10:24-25

Inspiring Worship

Gathering for worship is an uplifting and heart-stirring experience for the participants. The Holy Spirit is truly at work. The primary characteristic of worship is that it is God-centered—not self-centered.

Key question: Is the gathering for worship at our church an awe-inspiring experience focused on the presence and power of God?

References: Psalm 150:6; John 4:24; 1 Corinthians 14:24-25

Functional Structures

Organizational systems and procedures are suitable for the administration and governance of our church. Organizational structures are not tradition bound. They are adaptable and changeable to support the priorities and mission of the church.

Key question: Are the forms and methods of organization at our church established and evaluated in terms of their usefulness and effectiveness?

Reference: Acts 6:1-4

Passionate Spirituality

People have a joyful relationship with Jesus Christ and an abiding expectation that God will work in their midst. People are enthusiastic about sharing their faith with others.

Key question: Do the people who are part of our church live their faith with joy and share their faith with enthusiasm?

References: Matthew 22:37; Romans 12:1; Revelation 2:4-5

Relationship Evangelism

Our church focuses on already existing relationships rather than evangelism programs. People receive training for sharing their faith.

Key question: Are the people at our church intentional about sharing their faith with family and friends?

Reference: 1 Corinthians 9:20-22

notes

Introduction

1. Loren Mead, "Judicatory Interventions Can Help Small Congregations," in *New Possibilities for Small Churches,* ed. Douglas Alan Walrath (New York: Pilgrim, 1983), 87.
2. Kennon L. Callahan, *Small, Strong Congregations: Creating Strengths and Health for Your Congregation* (San Francisco: Jossey-Bass, 2000), 12–13.

Chapter 1: Why Smaller Is Better

1. George Barna, *The Second Coming of the Church: A Blueprint for Survival* (Nashville: Word, 1998), 16.
2. Ibid., 18.
3. Ibid., 93.
4. Ibid.
5. See *Experiencing God: How to Live the Full Adventure of Knowing and Doing the Will of God,* by Henry T. Blackaby and Claude V. King (Nashville: Broadman & Holman, 1994).
6. David R. Ray, *The Big Small Church Book* (Cleveland: Pilgrim, 1992), viii.
7. Ron Klassen and John Koessler, *No Little Places: The Untapped Potential of the Small-Town Church* (Grand Rapids, MI: Baker, 1996), 15.
8. Ray, *The Big Small Church Book,* 16–17.
9. See *Beyond the Ordinary: Ten Strengths of U.S. Congregations,* by Cynthia Woolever and Deborah Bruce (Louisville: Westminster John Knox, 2004).
10. Ibid., 135.

11. Ibid., 120.
12. Ibid., 20.
13. Ibid., 16, 38, 76, 94.

Chapter 2: Taking Your Church's Pulse

1. Barna, *The Second Coming of the Church,* 7.
2. "Day by Day—A Prayer," words by St. Richard of Chichester (1197–1253).
3. See 1 Corinthians 14:26-33; Colossians 3:16-17.
4. Ray, *The Big Small Church Book,* 12.
5. Os Guinness, *Dining with the Devil: The Megachurch Movement Flirts with Modernity* (Grand Rapids, MI: Baker, 1993), 77.
6. Ibid., 78.
7. Ray, *The Big Small Church Book,* 13.
8. See *Natural Church Development: A Guide to Eight Essential Qualities of Healthy Churches,* by Christian A. Schwarz (Carol Stream, IL: ChurchSmart Resources, 1996).
9. Christian A. Schwarz, "The Strong Little Church," *Leadership,* Fall 1999, 54.
10. Ibid.

Chapter 3: Shepherding

1. All of God's sheep, without exception, have gone astray (see Isaiah 53:6), and those who are in God's flock have returned to the same Shepherd (see 1 Peter 2:25).
2. Charles Jefferson, *The Minister as Shepherd* (Fort Washington, PA: Christian Literature Crusade, 1998), 66. Originally published by Thomas Y. Crowell, New York, 1912.
3. E. Glenn Wagner, *Escape from Church, Inc.: The Return of the Pastor-Shepherd* (Grand Rapids, MI: Zondervan, 1999), 10.
4. Ibid., 25, with modification.
5. Eugene H. Peterson, "To the Suburban Church of North America," *Christianity Today,* 25 October 1999, 67. Used by permission.

6. Susan Wise Bauer, "To the Rural Church," *Christianity Today,* 25 October 1999, 71. Used by permission.

7. John Piper, "Brothers, We Are Not Professionals," *The Standard,* November 1981, 43.

8. See *Wounded Workers: Recovering from Heartache in the Workplace and the Church,* by Kirk E. Farnsworth (Mukilteo, WA: WinePress, 1998).

9. Notice the contrast with the counterfeit shepherd in Revelation 13:11-18. All he can come up with is a number—the same one for everyone!

10. Jefferson, *The Minister as Shepherd,* 128.

Chapter 4: Gathering

1. Diana R. Garland, *Family Ministry: A Comprehensive Guide* (Downers Grove, IL: InterVarsity, 1999), 307.

2. Ray S. Anderson and Dennis B. Guernsey, *On Being Family: A Social Theology of the Family* (Grand Rapids, MI: Eerdmans, 1985), 38.

3. Rodney Clapp, *Families at the Crossroads: Beyond Traditional Roles and Modern Options* (Downers Grove, IL: InterVarsity, 1993), 101.

4. Garland, *Family Ministry,* 325.

5. Ron Owens, *Return to Worship: A God-Centered Approach* (Nashville: Broadman & Holman, 1999), 83-84.

6. See *Becoming a Shepherd: Contemporary Pastoral Ministry,* by Oliver McMahan (Cleveland, TN: Pathway, 1994).

7. Charles W. Colson, *The Body: Being Light in the Darkness* (Dallas: Word, 1992), 273.

8. Tim Stafford, "God Is in the Blueprints," *Christianity Today,* 7 September 1998, 77. Used by permission.

9. Ibid., 82.

10. Ibid.

Chapter 5: Covenanting

1. R. L. Honeycutt, "Risking the Arm," convocation address presented at Southern Baptist Theological Seminary, Louisville, KY, 1987. Quoted in Garland, *Family Ministry,* 358.

2. Colson, *The Body,* 276.

3. Ibid., 271.

4. These wonderfully descriptive expressions come from Bill Hybels's presentation at the Developing Today's Leaders Conference, City Bible Church, Portland, OR, March 2002.

5. Taken, with modification, from General Conference, Constitution of the Missionary Church (Fort Wayne, IN: Denominational Office, 1997), 33.

6. See *High Expectations: The Remarkable Secret of Keeping People in Your Church,* by Thom S. Rainer (Nashville: Broadman & Holman, 1999).

7. See *Church Discipline That Heals,* by John White and Ken Blue (Downers Grove, IL: InterVarsity, 1985). This is a compassionate book that counters abusive church discipline practices with Christlike practices calling for reconciliation, church purity, restoration of sinners, and freedom in Christ.

8. See *The Consumer Church: Can Evangelicals Win the World without Losing Their Souls?* by Bruce Shelley and Marshall Shelley (Downers Grove, IL: InterVarsity, 1992).

9. See *The Purpose-Driven Church: Growth without Compromising Your Message and Mission,* by Rick Warren (Grand Rapids, MI: Zondervan, 1995).

10. See "Game Plan: Leadership Training Supplement," in the 301 Depth Bible Study Series, published by Serendipity House, Littleton, CO.

11. Kingsley Fletcher, *The Power of Covenant* (Ventura, CA: Regal, 2000), 172–173.

12. Ibid., 179.

13. Larry Ocasio, "The Tithe: Our Covenant Privilege," *The Morning Star Journal,* vol. 11, no. 1, 32.

14. Colson, *The Body*, 376.

Chapter 6: Ministering

1. Gilbert Bilezikian, *Community 101: Reclaiming the Local Church as Community of Oneness* (Grand Rapids, MI: Zondervan, 1997), 11–12.

2. Roberta Hestenes, from the Foreword, in Greg Ogden, *The New Reformation: Returning the Ministry to the People of God* (Grand Rapids, MI: Zondervan, 1990), 7.

3. Ogden, *The New Reformation*, 75.

4. Ibid., 92.

5. Richard Lovelace, *Dynamics of Spiritual Life* (Downers Grove, IL: InterVarsity, 1979), 224. Quoted in Ogden, *The New Reformation*, 68.

6. Elton Trueblood, *The Best of Trueblood: An Anthology* (Nashville: Impact, 1979), 140. Quoted in Bill Hull, *The Disciple Making Pastor* (Grand Rapids, MI: Revell, 1988), 190.

7. Bilezikian, *Community 101*, 146.

8. See *The New Reformation*, by Greg Ogden.

9. Ibid., 86.

10. Ibid., 86–90, with modification.

11. Ibid., 91–94, with modification.

12. We are indebted to Ken Priddy for the discussion of the lifecycle of churches. Our information was received at the seminar titled "Church Redevelopment Training: How to Redevelop the Declining Church." Used by permission. For information about the seminar and church redevelopment resource materials contact the Church Multiplication Training Center, 3124 Summersworth Run, Ft. Wayne, IN 46804 (phone: 260/434-0090 or www.cmtcmultiply.org).

13. Warren, *The Purpose-Driven Church*, 368.

14. Bilezikian, *Community 101*, 90.

15. See *Planting Growing Churches for the 21st Century: A Comprehensive Guide for New Churches and Those Desiring*

Renewal, 2nd edition, by Aubrey Malphurs (Grand Rapids, MI: Baker, 1998).

16. Ibid., 161.
17. Warren, *The Purpose-Driven Church,* 384–385.

Chapter 7: Studying

1. A. W. Tozer, *Whatever Happened to Worship?* (Camp Hill, PA: Christian Publications, 1985), 94.
2. See *Educating for Responsible Action,* by Nicholas P. Wolterstorff (Grand Rapids, MI: Eerdmans, 1980).
3. Arthur Holmes, ed., *The Making of a Christian Mind* (Downers Grove, IL: InterVarsity, 1985), 18.
4. Ibid., 23–27, with modification. Used by permission.
5. See James H. Bryan, "How Adults Teach Hypocrisy," *Psychology Today,* December 1969, 50–74.
6. Steps developed from Wolterstorff, *Educating for Responsible Action,* 105.
7. Ibid., 65.
8. See *The Divine Conspiracy: Rediscovering Our Hidden Life in God,* by Dallas Willard (San Francisco: HarperSanFrancisco, 1998).
9. Ibid., 321.
10. Ibid., 322.
11. Quoted in Dean Merrill, "Not Married-with-Children," *Christianity Today,* 14 July 1997, 35.
12. See Andy Crouch, "Generation Misinformation," *Christianity Today,* 21 May 2001, 83.
13. Ibid.
14. Willard, *The Divine Conspiracy,* 343.
15. See the highly acclaimed *Celebration of Discipline: The Path to Spiritual Growth,* 3rd edition, by Richard J. Foster (San Francisco: HarperSanFrancisco, 1998).
16. Willard, *The Divine Conspiracy,* 354.

17. See *Shepherding the Small Church: A Leadership Guide for the Majority of Today's Churches,* by Glenn Daman (Grand Rapids, MI: Kregel, 2002), 253–254.

18. Willard, *The Divine Conspiracy,* 362.

Chapter 8: Worshiping

1. Willard, *The Divine Conspiracy,* 362–363.

2. See *Reaching Out without Dumbing Down: A Theology of Worship for the Turn-of-the-Century Culture,* by Marva J. Dawn (Grand Rapids, MI: Eerdmans, 1995).

3. Ibid., 24, 28, 64, 66.

4. See *Return to Worship,* by Ron Owens.

5. Dawn, *Reaching Out without Dumbing Down,* 109.

6. Ibid., 192.

7. Jefferson, *The Minister as Shepherd,* 29.

8. J. Daniel Baumann, "Worship: The Missing Jewel," *Christianity Today,* 21 November 1980, 28.

9. Bill Hull, *The Disciple Making Pastor* (Grand Rapids, MI: Fleming H. Revell, 1988), 96.

10. David C. Norrington, *To Preach or Not to Preach?* (Carlisle, UK: Paternoster, 1996), 8.

11. William D. Hendricks, *Exit Interviews: Revealing Stories of Why People Are Leaving the Church* (Chicago: Moody, 1993), 282–283.

12. Ibid., 284.

13. Dawn, *Reaching Out without Dumbing Down,* 238.

14. Ibid., 239.

15. Lawrence O. Richards, *A New Face for the Church* (Grand Rapids, MI: Zondervan, 1970), 148.

16. Norrington, *To Preach or Not to Preach?,* 115.

17. Ibid., 75–83.

18. Ibid., 69.

19. Joseph L. Garlington, *Worship: The Pattern of Things in Heaven* (Shippensburg, PA: Destiny Image, 1997), 8.

20. Dawn, *Reaching Out without Dumbing Down*, 88.

21. Ibid., 143, 153.

22. Richards, *A New Face for the Church*, 106, 108.

23. Hendricks, *Exit Interviews*, 260.

24. See *Real Worship: It Will Transform Your Life*, by Warren W. Wiersbe (Nashville: Oliver Nelson, 1990).

25. Owens, *Return to Worship*, 26.

Chapter 9: Praying

1. Dutch Sheets, *Intercessory Prayer* (Ventura, CA: Regal, 1996), 20.

2. S. D. Gordon, *Quiet Talks on Prayer* (New York: Grosset & Dunlap, 1941), 58–59.

3. Adapted from Fred A. Hartley III, "The Best Church Growth Method? Try Prayer," *Pray!*, July/August 1998, 22. Used by permission.

4. See *With Christ in the School of Prayer*, by Andrew Murray (Westwood, NJ: Fleming H. Revell, 1953).

5. Taken, with modification, from Alice Smith, "Praying Together: Annoying or Anointed?" *Pray!*, May/June 1998, 33–34. Used by permission.

6. Materials from "The Praying Church" by Sue Curran, copyright 1995 used by permission of Destiny Image Publishers, 167 Walnut Bottom Road, Shippensburg, PA 17257, www.destinyimage.com.

7. G. Campbell Morgan, *The Practice of Prayer* (Westwood, NJ: Fleming H. Revell, 1960), 120.

8. E. M. Bounds, *Purpose in Prayer*, new ed., (Grand Rapids, MI: Baker, 1991), 83–84.

9. Jack W. Hayford, *Prayer Is Invading the Impossible* (New York: Ballantine, 1977), 64.

10. Sheets, *Intercessory Prayer*, 208–209.

11. Charles Spurgeon, *The Power of Prayer in a Believer's Life* (Lynnwood, WA: Emerald, 1993), 192.

12. Sheets, *Intercessory Prayer*, 30, 29, 31, 32.

13. Ibid., 40.

14. See *Churches That Pray,* by C. Peter Wagner (Ventura, CA: Regal, 1993).

15. See *How Christians Can Join Together in Concerts of Prayer for Spiritual Awakening and World Evangelization,* by David Bryant (Ventura, CA: Regal, 1988).

16. See *Prayer Summits: Seeking God's Agenda for Your Community,* by Joe Aldrich (Portland, OR: Multnomah, 1992).

17. See *Churches That Pray,* by C. Peter Wagner, 167–185.

18. Elmer L. Towns, *Fasting for Spiritual Breakthrough* (Ventura, CA: Regal, 1996), 46.

19. Ibid., 73.

20. Foster, *Celebration of Discipline,* 54–55.

21. Ibid., 55.

22. Ibid.

23. Ibid., 56.

24. Hayford, *Prayer Is Invading the Impossible,* 59.

Chapter 10: Giving

1. Quoted in Ronald J. Sider, *Rich Christians in an Age of Hunger: Moving from Affluence to Generosity,* 4th ed. (Dallas: Word, 1997), 91.

2. See *The Spirit-Formed Church*, by Jack W. Hayford (Van Nuys, CA: Living Way Ministries, 2001). Used by permission.

3. Sider, *Rich Christians in an Age of Hunger,* 206.

4. Ibid., 241.

5. This list was taken from "Affluenza Viewer's Guide," courtesy of KCTS Television, Seattle, WA, 1997.

6. Adapted from "An Evangelical Commitment to Simple Lifestyle." Written and endorsed by the International Consultation on Simple Lifestyle, Hoddesdon, England, March 17–21, 1980, which was sponsored by the World Evangelical Fellowship Theological Commission's Unit on Ethics and Society and the Lausanne Committee on World Evangelization's Lausanne Theology and Education Group.

7. W. Ian Thomas, *The Saving Life of Christ* (Grand Rapids, MI: Zondervan, 1961), 43.

8. John V. Taylor, *Enough Is Enough: A Biblical Call for Moderation in a Consumer-Oriented Society* (Minneapolis: Augsburg, 1975), 85–88.

9. See *Experiencing God,* by Henry T. Blackaby and Claude V. King, 75–81.

10. Howard A. Snyder, *Liberating the Church: The Ecology of Church and Kingdom* (Eugene, OR: Wipf & Stock, 1996), 13.

11. Sider, *Rich Christians in an Age of Hunger,* 63.

Chapter 11: Living in the Spirit

1. Marva J. Dawn and Eugene H. Peterson, *The Unnecessary Pastor: Rediscovering the Call* (Grand Rapids, MI: Eerdmans, 2000).

2. Ibid., 129.

3. Ibid., 128.

4. Gordon D. Fee, *Paul, the Spirit, and the People of God* (Peabody, MA: Hendrickson, 1996), 127.

5. See 1 Samuel 2:3, Jeremiah 9:23-24 and 22:16, Micah 6:8, 1 Corinthians 1:31, and 2 Corinthians 10:17 and 12:9.

6. Jack W. Hayford, *Living the Spirit-Formed Life* (Ventura, CA: Regal, 2001), 8-9.

7. Ibid., 121–124.

8. Charles Stanley, *The Wonderful Spirit-Filled Life* (Nashville: Thomas Nelson, 1992), 108.

9. Ibid., 194.

10. Ibid., 204.

11. Ibid., 207.

12. Ibid., 210.

13. Ibid., 226.

14. Taken, with modification, from Ogden, *The New Reformation,* 14. Copyright © Greg Ogden. Used by permission.

15. Taken, with modification, from Hayford, *The Spirit-Formed Church* seminar, 7. Used by permission.

16. Howard A. Snyder, *The Problem of Wineskins: Church Structure in a Technological Age* (Downers Grove, IL: InterVarsity, 1975), 157.

Chapter 12: Witnessing

1. Tom Clegg and Warren Bird, *Lost in America: How You and Your Church Can Impact the World Next Door* (Loveland, CO: Group, 2001), 27.
2. Ibid., 33.
3. Ibid., 88. Quote is from Barna Research Group, "An Inside Look at Today's Churches Reveals Current Statistics on Protestant Churches," 30 October 1997.
4. Walter Brueggemann, *Biblical Perspectives on Evangelism: Living in a Three-Storied Universe* (Nashville: Abingdon, 1993), 130.
5. Ibid., 16–19, 43–47, 129–131.
6. We are indebted to Howard Snyder, *Liberating the Church,* for the concepts of disembodied gospel and disembodied Christ. (See pp. 152, 149.)
7. One of our basic beliefs is that before the return of Christ, there will be widespread persecution of Christ's followers. At the return of Christ, the Church will be removed and the wrath of God against unbelievers will begin. This view, referred to as the "pre-wrath rapture" view, uses Scripture to validate itself. Paul's use of "elect" for believers and Jesus' use of the word elect in Matthew 24:22 suggest that Jesus' followers will have to go through a time of great tribulation. "Those days" that Jesus refers to, however, cannot be the seven years mentioned in Revelation (see Daniel 9:27 and Revelation 11:2–3), but Jesus says that his followers will survive only if something that directly affects them is shortened—a tribulation of unknown length. Since God protects believers, while Satan hates them, we conclude that Satan will initiate this tribulation, yet Jesus will make it possible for Christians to proclaim salvation worldwide (Luke 21:10-19). This perspective motivates us to do all we can *now* so that more believers will be available to witness to

Christ, so there will be fewer people who have not heard and hence shorten the days of persecution. See Marvin Rosenthal, *The Pre-Wrath Rapture of the Church* (Nashville: Thomas Nelson, 1990), Robert D. Van Kampen, *The Sign* (Wheaton, IL: Crossway, 1992), and Robert D. Van Kampen, *The Rapture Question Answered: Plain and Simple* (Grand Rapids, MI: Fleming H. Revell, 1997) for more.

8. Dawn, *Reaching Out without Dumbing Down*, 50.

9. Used with permission from *Lost in America: How You and Your Church Can Impact the World Next Door*, by Tom Clegg & Warren Bird, published by group Publishing, Inc., PO Box 481, Loveland, CO 80539 www.group.com, 87–88.

10. See *Becoming a Contagious Christian*, by Bill Hybels and Mark Mittleberg (Grand Rapids, MI: Zondervan, 1994).

11. See *Nine Keys to Effective Small Group Leadership: How Lay Leaders Can Establish Dynamic and Healthy Cells, Classes, or Teams*, by Carl F. George (Mansfield, PA: Kingdom, 1997).

12. Schwarz, *Natural Church Development*, 47–48.

13. Ibid., 48.

14. Malphurs, *Planting Growing Churches for the 21st Century*, 25.

15. We are indebted to Michael Noel for these observations of the church plant at Antioch at the seminar titled "Bootcamp for Reproducing Churches." Used by permission. For information about the seminar or related materials, contact the Church Multiplication Training Center, 3124 Summersworth Run, Fort Worth, IN 46804 (phone: 206/434-0090 or www.cmtcmultiply.org).

16. Ibid.

17. Aubrey Malphurs, *Vision America: A Strategy for Reaching a Nation* (Grand Rapids, MI: Baker, 1994), 131.

18. We have taken these nine methods, with modification, from Noel, "Bootcamp for Reproducing Churches," Church Multiplication Training Center. Used by permission.

19. See Pam Mellskog, "Pursuing Community," *Vital Ministry*, March/April 1998, 49–52.

Appendix

1. Inspired by Schwarz, *Natural Church Development,* and Terry B. Walling and Gary B. Reinecke, *Assessing Your Church* (Anaheim: Church Resource Ministries, 1996). Information about resource materials for assessing the health of your church may be obtained from ChurchSmart Resources, 390 East Saint Charles Road, Carol Stream, IL 60188 (phone: 800/253-4276 or www.churchsmart.com).
2. The key indicator of church health.
3. The key indicator of church growth.

INDEX 1
small-church ADVANTAGES

Covenanting

Ministering

Studying

Worshiping

Praying

Giving

Living in the Spirit

Witnessing